REVOLUTIONARY PASSIONS

Some Books from Social Science Press and Aurum Books

Much Ado Over Coffee: Indian Coffee House Then and Now
BHASWATI BHATTACHARYA

Gitanjali Reborn: William Radice's Writings on Rabindranath Tagore
Edited by MARTIN KÄMPCHEN

Gandhi: Anti-biography of a Great Soul (HB)
MICHAEL DE SAINT-CHERON

Shades of Difference: Selected Writings of Rabindranath Tagore with Audio Visual Material, *Tagore and His World* (HB)
Edited by RADHA CHAKRAVARTY

Calcutta: The Stormy Decades (HB)
Edited by TANIKA SARKAR AND SEKHAR BANDYOPADHYAY

Dalit Women: Honour and Patriarchy in South India (HB)
CLARINDA STILL

Tamil Brahmans: The Creation of a Middle-Class Caste (HB)
CJ FULLER AND HARIPRIYA NARASIMHAN

Persistence of Poverty in India (HB)
Edited by NANDINI GOOPTU AND JONATHAN PARRY

Savage Attack: Tribal Insurgency in India (HB)
Edited by CRISPIN BATES AND ALPA SHAH

The Year of Blood: Essays on the Revolt of 1857 (HB)
RUDRANGSHU MUKHERJEE

The Autobiography of a Revolutionary in British India (HB)
KALI GHOSH

The Many Worlds of Sarala Devi: A Diary
Translated by SUKHENDU RAY and
The Tagores and Sartorial Styles: A Photo Essay (HB)
MALAVIKA KARLEKAR

Viramma: Life of a Dalit (PB)
VIRAMMA, JOSIANE RACINE, AND JEAN-LUC RACINE

Everyday Nationalism: Women of the Hindu Right (HB)
KALYANI DEVAKI MENON

Marriage, Love, Caste & Kinship Support: Lived Experiences of the Urban Poor in India (HB)
SHALINI GROVER

Religious Division and Social Conflict: The Emergence of Hindu Nationalism in Rural India (PB)
PEGGY FROERER

Literature and Nationalist Ideology: Writing Histories of Indian Languages (PB)
HANS HARDER

The Everyday State and Society in Modern India (PB)
Edited by CJ FULLER AND VERONIQUE BENEI

Economics and Its Stories (HB)
AMAL SANYAL

Telecommunications Industry in India: State Business and Labour in a Global Economy (HB)
DILIP SUBRAMANIAM

Cultural History of Modern India (PB)
Edited by MEENAKSHI KHANNA

Income Poverty and Beyond: Human Development in India
Edited by RAJA J CHELLIAH AND R SUDARSHAN

The Politics of the Pharmaceutical Industry and Access to Medicines: World Pharmacy and India (HB)
Edited by HANS LOGREN

SERIES: EVERYDAY LIFE OF POLITICAL STRUGGLES

Windows into a Revolution: Ethnographies of Maoism in India and Nepal (HB)
Edited by ALPA SHAH AND JUDITH PETTIGREW

Rebels from the Mud Houses: Dalits and the Making of the Maoist Revolution in Bihar (HB)
GEORGE KUNNATH

Unruly Hills: Nature and Nation in India's North-East (HB)
BENGT G. KARLSSON

SERIES: GERMAN WRITINGS ON INDIA AND SOUTH ASIA

'When the war began we heard of several kings': South Asian Prisoners in World War I Germany (HB)
Edited by FRANSIZKA ROY, HEIKE LIEBAU AND RAVI AHUJA

Cultural Encounters in India: The Local Co-Workers of the Tranquebar Mission, 18th-19th Centuries (HB)
HEIKE LIEBAU

'Everwhere is Becoming the Same'? Regulating IT-work between India and Germany (HB)
NICOLE MAYER-AHUJA

SERIES: FRENCH WRITINGS ON INDIA AND SOUTH ASIA

Scholars and Prophets: Sociology of India from France in the 19th and 20th Centuries (HB)
ROLAND LARDINOIS

Tocqueville in India (HB)
JEAN ALPHONSE BERNARD

AURUM BOOKS

Sabotage (PB)
ANITA AGNIHOTRI
Translated by ARUNAVA SINHA

Opium Poppy (PB)
HUBERT HADDAD
Translated by RENUKA GEORGE

Forthcoming titles from SSP

From 'People' to 'Citizen': Democracy's Must Take Road (HB)
DIPANKAR GUPTA

Society and Culture in India (PB)
Edited by SUBAS MOHAPATRA

French Writings on India and South Asia

REVOLUTIONARY PASSIONS

LATIN AMERICA, MIDDLE EAST AND INDIA

by
Hamit Bozarslan, Gilles Bataillon
and Christophe Jaffrelot

Translated from the French by
Soma Datta Gupta

SOCIAL
SCIENCE
PRESS

Published by
Esha Béteille
Social Science Press
69 Jor Bagh, New Delhi 110003

Editions de l'EHESS
105, boulevard Raspail,
75006 Paris, France
www.editions.ehess.fr

The Work is published via the Publication Assistance Programme Tagore, with the support of the Institut Français en Inde/Ambassade de France en Inde and the Institut Français de Paris.

ISBN: 978-93-83166-17-6

Set in Sabon Lt Std 10.5/14
Typeset by Manmohan Kumar, Delhi 110035
Printed by Vee Enn Print-O-Pac
A-5, Flatted Factory Complex, Okhla Industrial Estate Ph-III
New Delhi - 110020

Contents

Protesters on Avenue Habib Bourguiba, downtown Tunis on 14 January 2011, a few hours before President Zine El Abidine Ben Ali fled the country.

Source: https://en.wikipedia.org/wiki/Arab_Spring#/media/File:Tunisia_Unrest_-_VOA_-_Tunis_14_Jan_2011_(2).jpg

Introduction

Hamit Bozarslan

Tunis, 13 January, 2011; President Zine el Abidine Ben Ali tells his countrymen that he has been kept in the dark about the riots shaking the country since 17 December and was totally unaware of how serious the situation was. The President also promises that he would not contest for the post of the President for the sixth time in 2014.

Tunis, 14 January, 2011: President Zine el Abidine Ben Ali boards a presidential aircraft and flees the country in the cover of darkness shortly before the airports are sealed off.

Very recently, Tunisia, an African country, experienced, within a span of just 24 hours, as many as four political trials. While on 14 January 2011, the riots shook Tunis itself for the third consecutive day, thus confirming that the country was passing through a revolutionary crisis, the struggle for power between the two leaders – the head of State, Major Rachid Anwar and President Ben Ali took the form of a palace coup. To these two was added a third trial, some kind of a political restoration since, following the dramatic turn of events taking place on a single day, the President of the National Assembly, Fouad Mbazaa, became the interim President of the country and entrusted Mohammed Ghannouchi, former Prime Minister of Ben Ali, with the responsibility of forming a new government. The fourth and the final event was that while these two trusted right hand men of Ben Ali no longer dared to influence him in any matter, the earlier regime unleashed terror by the parallel security services that became its final footprint.

In the past, a political chronology was rarely crammed with so many simultaneous political processes. But the Tunisian revolt also had some other distinctive features of its own. While the Islamists, who often occupied important positions in the Arab world during the last ten decades, did not feature anywhere on the scene, the ongoing political unrest, mobilized the marginalized section of the people in the suburban towns, like Sidi Bouzid, Kasserine, Thala or Regueb, before capturing the capital just three days before the fall of the Leader. Triggered by the public display of self-immolation of the young, educated but unemployed Mohammed Boazizi, it was a riot of bread and wheelbarrow before it became an uprising of intellectuals. In the face of this tumultuous protest movement, the men in power could not this time resort to force as heavily as it did in 1984 (when 150 people were killed, in Tunis alone); moreover, in spite of its self-confessed illegality, the regime pleaded with the people to bring it back to power for one last time till 2014 and condemned itself, in just a few hours, to become 'an Ancien régime' (former regime). 'Misfortune to the elites in power who admit their weakness', said Pareto. In doing so, the regime also demonstrated that in the final analysis, it managed to maintain an 'artificial equilibrium' by an 'illusion of power' as the theorists of the Latin American fiery revolutionaries (fuegos) would have said, since it was no longer capable of mobilizing on a long-term basis its para governmental militia and even less its army.

Contrary to the great revolutions of the past, French, Russian or Iranian, the Tunisian protest movement did not brandish the 'bloody flag' against its oppressors because it went hand in hand, in its initial days at least, with a palace coup and a restoration. But it showed to what extent, from then on, it was the common men in the street and not power, alone, who had the right to define friends and foes, as well as one exacting penalty and vengeance.

The common men, who took up the visible space which was till recently, occupied entirely by the men in power (and the tourists), put up a united front against the 'body' of the State by mobilizing themselves and by their determination to overcome fear. Here, as in the other revolutionary contexts one witnessed the emergence of a regime of intense subjectivity, serious and dark, awaiting an imminent liberation.

This event, not only unpredictable but also dramatic, which took the observers by surprise, justifies in itself its inclusion in this book dedicated to revolutionary passions. Coordinated by one of his former students, the initial aim of the project (and we hope to have partially succeeded) was, to propose a series of lectures in the form of a posthumous dialogue with François Furet, ranging from, on the one hand, his *Past of an Illusion*, published in 1994, and, on the other, to the non-European worlds, shaken all through the twentieth century, by their hopes, passions and revolutionary crises.

As it would strike the reader, our objective was not to test the validity of the reflections of Furet elsewhere in the world, but to extend the debate taking it beyond the communist involvement strictly within the confines of Europe. We shall thus try to provide answers to a series of questions relevant as much to the specialists of the 'cultural school' as to those in the domain of comparative linguistics. To what extent have the revolutionary experiences of the 'Tri-Continent' been influenced by the European matrix which they refer to? Have they, in their turn, given rise to exportable models? How do we understand the revolutionary passions, not only of the Left but also of the nationalists or the Right, born outside the European continent?

To answer these questions, it is necessary first of all, to make a distinction between the revolutionary passions and hopes on the one hand and on the other, the revolution as the theatre of unpredictable action, deriving its meanings from its very own dynamics and internal chronology.

If revolutionary passions could be observed over a long period and replicated through a plurality of channels, from exodus, quasi-religious movements, likely to lead to millenarian protest movements[1] to the propagation of loaded statements with hidden transcripts[2], from the philosophical criticism of power to subversive artistic creation. But for all that they do not explain the process of radicalization, of polarization and in certain cases also of militarization of revolutionary theatres that can only be understood when viewed on a narrow temporal scale. But this distinction is equally heuristic, involving trial and error, for another reason. A number of societies are, in fact, shaped by the hope of a revolutionary rupture, even of a 'final battle' marking the end of history which however is not translated necessarily by a revolutionary episode as one would observe in France, Russia or Iran. As the history of Europe of the twentieth century shows, revolutionary commitment can also dissociate itself from revolutionary axiology to give birth to counter societies, to dissident forces of opposition, more or less regulated, or to circles of autonomous socialization. The 'revolutionary sacrifice', another name for commitment may subsequently be translated by an outpouring of solidarity towards revolutionary experiences, which have become a myth, functioning in certain societies.

Secondly, one is at a loss as to how to analyse revolutionary passions and commitments from a comparative perspective. Certainly, Europe, the principal field of study of François Furet, remains the centre stage of revolutionary passions and activities. In fact, even if each period, historical cycle and the European space has to be studied individually and the discontinuities of each country are to be taken into consideration, nothing would stop us from thinking that the post-1789 European radicalism is a part

[1] Vittorio Lantenari, *Les mouvements religieux des peoples opprimés*, Paris, La Découverte, 1983.

[2] James C. Scott, *La domination et les arts de la résistance: fragments du discours subalterne*, Paris, Éditions Amsterdam, 2009.

of the integrated history of the continent. Beyond the inevitable imaginary politics on which it thrives this reference legitimizes not only the revolutionary passions of the Left in Europe but also, implicitly, the counter-revolutions or the conservative revolutions which take a stand primarily against her.

Can one for all that, analyse revolutionary passions in a single, specific historical context and call it entirely European? In reality, and in all respects, the history of Europe of the last two centuries merges with 'world history' partly because, throughout its colonial history, Europe was the dominant power in the world, but partly also because its revolutionary experiences and references had become universal, serving as sources of inspiration to radical protests elsewhere. Such an approach, which suggests the existence of a second integrated history of the world, does not of course signify that the political culture, the State doctrine commanding the submission of the subjects to the Leader, or the imaginary local protesters pushing them towards revolt, fade away to make room for a sterilized bland global revolutionary matrix, bearing the European mark.

We hope to have showed that while playing the role of a filter, slowing down the diffusion of European revolutionary ideas or, to put it the other way round, facilitating their reception by their permeability, these local references could not put up a strong defence in the face of the universalization of revolutionary passions.

One must keep in mind that this movement of universalization was not at all unique. It is therefore appropriate to emphasize the paradox of the October Revolution which was fully integrated with the history of Europe in the sense that it was the direct result of a war involving the continent as a whole. But at the same time, it marked the displacement of the revolutionary reference beyond Berlin, considered till then as much as the limit of Europe than as one of its standard bearer revolutionaries. The fact that the first socialist revolution took place in Russia, 'a backward country', still dominated by the 'Asiatic shadows', and not in western Europe, did not only surprise the European socialists like Karl Kautsky or Rosa Luxemburg, but also provoked a major epistemological rupture within the Bolshevik party itself. It was a rupture which was overcome only by the elimination of half of the party leaders in the 1930s and in the Gulag. Nevertheless, the Left revolutionaries of Europe, then in the interim period between the two World Wars, evolved in certain countries such as France and Italy under the ideological (and sometimes organic) control of a revolutionary reference, which some would consider Asian. Closer to us in history, we see to what extent the Maoism of the Cultural Revolution, although profoundly related to the Chinese experience, exercised considerable influence among European intellectuals.

Rather than covering this universal history in all its complexities, our aim was to shed light on one particular aspect – revolutionary passions. We did not wish to impose a definitive set of guidelines for the understanding of the contributions on Latin America, the Middle East and India. Written in the form of essays, each contribution has, in fact, provided a key to the understanding of the subject, starting on a temporal scale thought appropriate. We, however hope that the project begun here will not confine itself to this single volume and that other, more extensive initiatives, will follow.

20 January 2011

François Furet (1927–97), historiographer of the French Revolution

Source: https://www.wikiberal.org/wiki/Fran%C3%A7ois_Furet

chapter 1

François Furet: *The Past of an Illusion* and the Revolutionary Enigma

Hamit Bozarlan

Before analysing the contribution of *The Past of an Illusion* by François Furet to the understanding of revolutionary passions and phenomena, let us briefly explain how we will read the text and then locate the context in which it was written.

One should make it clear at the outset that while the *Past* is considered a 'stand-alone' work, since it deals with a particular topic, and provides the framework and appropriate arguments, to understand the role of the French Revolution, it cannot be separated from Furet's entire body of work on the 20th century. A number of ideas developed in depth in the *Past* are, in fact, implicit, sometimes as sub-text in previous studies. This continuity makes inevitable the journeys back and forth in an exhaustive work produced over four decades.

Without underrating this work, the present contribution does not wish, however, to reproduce Furet's interpretation (or rather interpretations) of the revolutionary phenomenon.[1] Starting from the approach he develops, we would rather place the revolutionary passions and phenomena – two subjects of complementary

[1] As an example, we shall not by any means insist here on his famous interpretation of 1789 where he refers to the similarities between the Ancien Régime and the Revolution but unlike Tocqueville, underlines more what is completely unique about the latter.

research but nevertheless distinct – as 'enigmas' of social science. We are aware of the risks of such a decision; it inevitably puts the work being analysed under critical observation and it leads, to its conclusion, by translating it into a language which is not at all that of the author.

Furet who is the interpreter, engaged in analysing two revolutions of universal significance, suggests a series of guardrails for his readers. We hope that we will not be doing him a disservice when we say that the comparison between 1789 and 1917, whether explicit or implicit, is only a valid exercise if it serves to fathom what in fact radically differentiates the two revolutions.

We shall return to this point in greater detail; here we shall only point out that this unique character of the two revolutions does not mean that there was no link between them. It is evident, for example, that the Russian Revolution was born in a Europe, reconfigured by the French Revolution. Similarly, there is absolutely no doubt that the people of 1917 are cast in the imagination of those of 1789 to the point of having 'acquired the power to play any role that the great drama of history would assign them, and in case there is no role other than that of a traitor, they would rather accept it with enthusiasm in order to be a part of the spectacle'.[2] Getting back to the Russian Revolution, it could not exercise a similar 'charm', particularly in France, simply because it was able to capitalize on the prestige that the 'Mother-Revolution' of 1789 conferred on it. What Alphonse Aulard, renowned historian and activist of human rights and democracy, 'compares, what he defends in the two revolutions, the French and the Russian', says Furet, 'is simply that they are not comparable on a philosophical plane. It is quite simply that they are both revolutions' (XX S, 587). In spite of these links, established by authorization or revolutionary fetishism, 1917 remains specific for its context, autonomous in its dynamics and in its apathy which will, eventually lead it to scuttle

[2] Hannah Arendt, *Essai sur la revolution*, Paris, Gallimard, 1967, p. 80.

it. In continuation of this argument, I would like to add that if the French Revolution offers a referential matrix to a number of revolutions or drastic change of regimes across the world, it does not hold the 'code' of intelligibility, either of its entire history or of one of its episodes, constituting the Republican, Terrorist, Thermidorian, Brumarian, or even the Warrior.

For Furet, a revolution is first a social and a political phenomenon; in other words, by the plurality of interpretations that it makes possible, by the complexity of the field of research that it offers, it exercises a renewed fascination for successive generations of researchers. Turning to concepts like *fact* or *enigma*, constitutes in itself a double invitation: it revives, on the one hand, the necessity to historicize each and every revolution (XXS, 397); on the other, it emphasizes that to arrive there, one must first proceed towards a 'complexity of implementation'[3], consequently liberating the historical reading from both the philosophy of history, and from the 'religion of history' (XXS, 981).[4] There is no doubt that each revolution enables one to understand, starting with the crisis it is born of, the power structures and modes of legitimization of the previous regime that it overthrows, but none has the authority to disclose the future historical plan, national or universal.

If revolutions, observed over time and in more than one region share overall features such as contesting political legitimacy and

[3] On this theme, see Jacques Revel (ed.), *Jeux d'échelles. La micro-analyse à l'expérience*, Paris, Gallimard-Le Seuil-Éditions de l'EHESS, 1998, coll. "Hautes Études".

[4] Surely, for Furet, the battle against historicism is first a challenge for the social sciences: 'It is no longer about the historicist history which makes the temporal scale, the principle of the progress of humanity, nuanced by the formation of the nation states and the extension of "civilization", that is to say, of the European model. Today, on the contrary, the characteristic of history is not to be loaded any more with a meaning, preliminary and implicit, given to time and to break away from this linear vision which had made it, in a highly disciplined manner, responsible for weighing the merits of the different "periods" of the past' (A, 10).

establishing countervailing powers based on street force, and they seem to give grounds to understand them through a stereotypical trajectory, they still fail to follow any law of universal historical necessity; nor can they, even taken as a whole, offer readers any keys to understand better the 'evolution of humanity'.

Therefore to question revolution, positions it among in the range of issues covered by the social sciences. The act of revolution offers a chance to social scientists to understand concepts such as breakdown or rupture or the undefined. As Peter Berger, one of the greatest present-day sociologists, clarifies, which I interpret here somewhat freely before citing it in the margin, the social sciences are assigned the task of comprehending and explaining the established order, known as the authority, where every institution rests upon regulated power structures.[5]

The Social Sciences which have their origins in positivism face difficulties in grasping radical de-reglementation or rupture in situations where authority itself dissolves or where submission ceases to be a *habitus*, where the new builds on a movement not controlled by a single actor; when coercion and violence can co-exist within one single act. Despite so much ambiguity and contradiction and indecision, these can also end by launching *processes* and opening up a 'new order'. The work of Furet is interesting in this particular study, as it helps in the understanding of these complex processes.

FURET'S PASSION

As to the context of the writing of the *Past*, one must, first of all, find out the reasons that prompted a chronicler of the French Revolution to embark on a subject as difficult as communism and

[5] "The fundamental problem of sociology is not the crime but the law, not the divorce but the marriage, not the racial discrimination but the racial stratification, not the revolution but the government", Peter L. Berger, *Invitation to Sociology. A Humanistic Perspective*, New York-London-Toronto, Anchor Books, 1994, p. 130.

to devote his time to produce a work, that was, to use one of his cherished expressions, 'written somewhat haphazardly' (écrit à la diable). A second question also comes up: why does his book intend to cover so many subjects – from the establishment of the Soviet system to the internal history of Bolshevism, from the history of totalitarianism to the cowardice of the democracies, as during the Spanish Civil War, from the generations of Europeans committed to defending the USSR to the hopes it aroused far beyond Marxist circles?

Three additional answers seem possible here. In the first place, let us keep in mind that for, Furet, as for Tocqueville – who, along with Françoise Mélonio, wrote the preface to his book – studying history 'is studying politics by other means' (T, IX). The 'journalistic' texts he wrote from the 50s till the end (of his life), indeed, prove that he was passionate about politics, however, unlike his distant predecessor, he had absolutely no plan of making a career out of it.) Addressing these and other questions in this work, he was, so to say, in 'his element'. In the second place, as he himself makes it clear in his preface, with *The Past*, Furet puts an end to a personal experience, several decades old, marked alternately by commitment within the Communist Party, before distancing himself because of dissension and finally, a complete break from the communist tradition. But the third reason, which appears central to us, and which pushed him to engage himself in this huge task, rested in his passionate desire to urgently address this topic. The 'Communist ideal', so evident till just yesterday, was destined for a terrifying decline from (1989–91), and its critics, on the right, and one often forgets, on the left, had already become largely inaudible. Since the short turning point of this decade, indeed, the specialists had to mobilize all the resources hermeneutics had to offer in order to grasp the evolution of the communist syntax during the 20th century. Furet felt the urgent need to write on the significance of the 'Communist ideal' – on how much it had meant just a short time back, and how it could become so insignificant in a relatively short period.

Furet is one of the rare intellectuals we know to give such a lot of importance to paradoxes, and as a serious student of Tocqueville, to put himself in a paradoxical methodological position in order to be able to make them meaningful.[6] This approach is increased twofold and is made complex by the relations of proximity and distance that it maintains with its subject. He is an eminent member of a generation of historians who had the 'happy life', at least on the professional and intellectual plane (A5), but he is not an 'authorized' historian of his subject. He is familiar with the thoughts and work of a number of contemporary Left thinkers of the century about whom he speaks with fascination and sometimes also with admiration (Rosa Luxemburg, Georg Lukács ...), but he is no longer the player of the history that he traces. He retains the orientation, shared by so many friends and colleagues (XXS, 512)[7] of 'having lived in an illusion', but the historian also knows well that it was this illusion that produced a reality.

It mobilized more than a generation of supporters, coming from diverse backgrounds, who helped in the formation of social circles, in the elaboration of a tradition, both militant and intellectual, a way of thought, a *habitus* that compelled hundreds of thousands of people across the world to sacrifice their lives for the cause.

The tensions that are there throughout *The Past* from the beginning to the end are, therefore, as much the internal tensions of the man as those of his subject. To understand them, it would

[6] See, for an overall view of his work, Ran Halévy, *L'expérience du passé. Francois Furet dans l'atelier de l'histoire*, Paris, Gallimard, 2007; Pierre Hassner, "François Furet et le liberalism mélancolique", *in* XXS, pp. ix–xxiii; Mona Ozouf, "François Furet, comment écrire la revolution", *in* RF, pp. i–xxvi.

[7] In his response to the criticism of E. Hobsbawm, Furet makes it clear that this other historian of the *extremes* 'does not accept the idea that there was a communist illusion and, therefore, the very subject of my work appears to him to be unfamiliar'. (XXS, 461).

be proper to put oneself, if only for a moment, in this incredible period that began in 1989 with the fall of the communist regimes in East Europe and closed with the banning of the Communist Party in the USSR (which bourgeois democracy would have dared this act?) followed by the dissolution of the Empire in 1991. Whether they were cynics or sincere, henceforth, no one in Moscow finds in the doctrine of struggle on which had founded a system, *their* system, anything but a lie. The Communist parties, these 'wholesale grocers' and 'brand ambassadors', specializing in 'one single dish' regarding their interpretation of Soviet history (XXS, 317) did not allow for the legacy of a past so closely linked to Moscow.

The acknowledgement of illusion is, therefore, unanimous within the communist camp. Certainly, the historian's work begins only after the strong verdict of those who are personally interested. Once it is accepted, it is the duty of the historian to get back to the 'real', in other words, to the 'experience' of this 'illusion', to construct it as a subject of research and then to understand it, starting from the *present* as well as the *past*. But, these two periods of time have never appeared as Siamese twins. Rendering it meaningless, the present eats into the past which, for the historian, still remains overloaded with meaning. Far from signifying an end to the revolution[8], it merrily demolishes the edifice constructed by its immediate past (XXS, 510) and, flushed with an euphoric sentiment worthy of revolutionary intoxication, the people of East Europe celebrate the 'pure negation of the times they have lived through' (XXS, 415). All reference to socialism disappears by itself to make way for a deafening, even shameless homage, of capitalism, held in contempt only till the other day. On the one hand, the withering of the past has such a searing intensity

[8] Furet situates the exit of the October Revolution as the passage to Stalinism which, while deifying the Party, thus marks the end of the 'first Bolshevism' (XXS,661).

that one cannot even talk about a past regime[9]; on the other, the history of the 20th century is likely to become purely and simply absurd if one glosses over it.

It is precisely this paradox that Furet grapples with. His ambition is not to bring out a *black list* that would refer to a *reified* 'communism', free from all burden, historical, social, economic, as being responsible for all the misery of mankind from Cambodia to Ethiopia. Seen from this perspective, one cannot agree with the remark of Enzo Traverso[10]: '*The Past of an Illusion* reveals the arrogance of the conqueror, *The Age of the Extremes* is written by someone, defeated, who does not renounce his fight. Contrary to the opinion of several commentators, the melancholy, the legacy of a century of lost battles tinge the pages of Hobsbawm, not those of Furet [...]. Furet wrote in defence of liberal capitalism; Hobsbawm wrote a melancholic apology of communism'.

One does not need to recall Furet's powerful commentaries on 'liberal capitalism'. The reader will easily find them in the two collections used in this article. One must, on the other hand, make it clear that, along with a reading of *The Past*, from the perspective of the political right, a simultaneous reading from the left is also possible, as in his writings Furet relies heavily on the criticisms that a number of dissident intellectuals directed at the USSR in the 20th century. Moreover, Furet, like Hobsbawm, unanimously regarded as one of the greatest historians of our time, as are a number of other intellectual figures, from Aron, who was only marginally involved with the Left, to Bourdieu, who never broke away with the Left, and lived through the 20th century in

[9] Let us also remember that at the same time, the repression of the student movement in China shows the brutality 'the communist regime' is capable of; but, henceforth the Communist Party, in fact, succeeds in leading this vast country only because of the resources provided by an unbridled capitalism and an exclusive socialism.

[10] Enzo Traverso, "Le siècle de Hobsbawm", *La Revue internationale des livres et des idées*, no. 10, 2009, p. 14.

its quasi-totality or in the second half refusing to give in to any kind of cynicism, ... A reflexive rupture, and state of permanent 'disquiet', which renders them the honourable members of a single community in our eyes.

REVOLUTION AS A HEURISTIC SUBJECT FOR RESEARCH IN THE SOCIAL SCIENCES

One shall not insist here on the plurality of meaning that the term *revolution* implies. For the sake of convenience, we shall define it as a long-lasting crisis of governance, where an established power loses its legitimacy as it is no longer in a position to command submission from its subjects and, conversely, where a number of actors, without any institutional legitimacy, have their say in the matter, elaborate historical narratives in contradiction to the discourse of power and gradually install a de facto authority, before making it institutional, when a revolution takes place on the streets. To paraphrase Lenin, the revolutionary moment defines this situation as one where the earlier (order) no longer functions and the new one is not yet in place. The palaces are still occupied by the rightful holders of the title but without any power to command: the street holds the de facto power but it has not yet besieged the palace.

Starting from this narrow definition that the following pages would examine in more detail and bring out the finer aspects in the light of the reflections of Furet, one can put forward two hypotheses. In the first place, the more the crises of legitimacy of an established power, including the ones in the democratic regimes, are frequent, the more the revolutionary crises, seen as complex and indeterminate processes, are exceptional. In the second place, it would be proper, in the long history of revolutions[11], to differentiate the 'model revolutions', which can be 'universalized', because they

[11] See Jim DeFronzo, *Revolutionary Movements in World History. From 1750 to the Present*, Santa Barbara, ABC Clio, 2006, 3 vol.

can usher in the hope of an emancipation beyond the national or territorial boundaries, of those (who are) inspired by them. These model revolutions are also distinct from the conservative or nationalist revolutions of the 20th century (including fascism in Italy that Furet rightly analyses as a full-fledged revolution).

The number of 'model-revolutions', having at the same time a tragic but vain wish to be exported abroad and a universal appeal that make them 'exportable', would be limited, in our opinion, to three: French, Russian and Iranian. The first designates, according to Furet, 'the history of this French Constitution as body politic' (T, X, LVII). If it fails to go beyond its frontier, in ways other than through revolutionary war, it constitutes a historic landmark in the European context and becomes the founding reference of numerous protest movements in the 19th and 20th centuries. In spite of the considerable influence that it exerts in Europe and the constitution of the International, agents of dissemination worldwide, the second, the Soviet, is fast 'nationalized' and everything 'is brought under state control'. In Furet's interpretation, it appears equally fruitless in the long run, as the system it establishes disappears without leaving behind a legacy accepted by a society that it had nonetheless entirely shaped. Finally, the Iranian Revolution of which Furet does not offer, as far as we know, any interpretation, may be singularized by its socially conservative aspect owing to the participation of the *bazaris* and by its open link with religion which does not however explain its overall dynamics. It redefines the universal by reducing it drastically, by limiting it exclusively to the Islamic world, for which it sets itself up as a model. That is why it is placed somewhere between the revolutions extolling the emancipation of humanity and the nationalist revolutions of the Right. There is absolutely no doubt that it is institutionalized with the setting up of a coercive order and of a political system, allowing some internal political pluralism. Contrary to the experience of the Soviet Union, it allows a certain interpretive pluralism of its own history. In the final analysis, in other words, when serious crises occur, the regime's armed militants, and the anti-West and anti-Semitist interpretations, potentially millenarian, of the world that provide it stable resources.

THE WAR OF 1914–18

The Suicide of the Bourgeois Republican State and the Revolutionary Phenomenon

One of the most gripping chapters of the *Past* is not about the revolutionary phenomenon as such, but the Great War. The reason for this choice is simple but there is a long history behind it. The War of 1914–18 is a betrayal of the bourgeois society itself, and thus prepares the conditions that trigger the revolutionary dynamics which threaten it. On this point Furet is, in fact, placed on the same wave length as those historians who see in the War of 1914–18, firstly, a new episode of the brutalization of European societies and an organized violence on a scale thus far not known. It is only by the imprint that it leaves on European space and time that the War transforms the revolutionary imagination and expectations; it condemns the revolutions of the 20th century to being entirely different from the emancipatory ones of the 18th and 19th centuries. In spite of the horror of the Terror, of the extravaganza of the 18th Brumaire and the Empire which follows it, the French Revolution, leads Furet to recall in detail, time and time again, of the construction of a complex political society, conflicting but viable (or inversely, it is viable because it is conflicting). It does not only mark the 'birth of democracy' but even illustrates 'the tensions and the contradictory passions linked to this hitherto unseen condition of man as a social being' (XXS, 545). In spite of their failures and the repressions that follow, the insurrections of 1848 contribute to the democratization of a part of Europe under autocratic monarchies. Inversely, it is Furet's idea, not his expression, that the revolutions of the 20th century have an element of politicide, as they lead to *organicist* societies, aiming at eliminating all conflicts like division and enmity.

One of the reasons compelling Furet to emphasize the role of the War of 1914–18 is undoubtedly the uneasy relationship fostered by the French Left. On the one hand, it has always disliked it and in short have explained it from the Leninist perspective as an imperialist conflict that aimed to divide up the world; on the other hand it could not ignore the fact (and this included the communist constituents) that the War formed part of a nation's history, where boundaries between the particular and the universal, between sacrifice for the nation and for humanity remained relatively hazy. The second reason that interested Furet was that the French victory in 1918 was only the victory of the Third French Republic, which had been founded after the defeat of the 1871 against Prussia and which collapsed after a new defeat against Germany at the beginning of the Second World War; thus, it straddled the borderline that distinguished tyranny from democracy, to the point of draining the latter of its substance.

Indeed, the War 'signifies the end of the citizen but it is so difficult to put an end to the War only because it is democratic [...], the sufferings have been so painful, the deaths so many that no one dares act as if these were not essential' (EH, 44). The democratization of the War in the sense that it is practically approved by all and led by the elected representatives of the nation, does not prevent it from causing destruction to civilization (XXS, 570) and to the state, first, in so far as it is synonymous with the bourgeois *order*, then, in so far as it is challenged in this capacity by a socialist movement with universal aspirations. The protestors of the bourgeois state in the name of a wider fraternity, that of the proletariat, participate as much in destroying the state as the bourgeoisie itself. It is a historic retreat not only from their objectives but also from the universal Enlightenment of Europe. Finally, the participation of the Socialists and the Social Democrats in the War provokes, *a posteriori,* an exceptional phenomenon of 'repression', that does not fail to make a comeback in the form of the Congress of Tours (25–30 December 1920) during which the French Communist Party has been founded, and the apparition of a pro-Soviet Left elsewhere.

As Furet shows, before being a source of hope for millions of people outside Russia, the October Revolution constitutes a radical break in the rationale for the 'Sacred Union', through which the German, Austrian and French left-wing parties accepted to vote the 'war budgets' proposed by their respective governments (XXS, 602), thus reminding the European Left of their betrayal of 1914.

In the light of these facts, it is clear why Furet is so preoccupied with this War and tries hard to understand how Europe could do 'that' before analysing how this 'that' could radically reconfigure Europe. In this context, he cites Élie Halévy who considers the peace of 1918 to be a simple truce with barbarism, since the dynamics unleashed by the War evade the control of the legal authorities of the countries involved (EH, 52–54). Far from indicating the return to the bourgeois republican state, spread over the whole of the continent as if the War had never taken place, peace transforms Europe into a field open to all axiological investment. While organizing itself for several years around the War, in other words, putting aside the bourgeois order, the (Republican) state destroyed its ability to project itself into a peaceful future, the right to construct a new society by action and violence is largely democratized; the methods of 'propaganda', this 'Rape of the Masses'[12] to which States had heavily resorted to during the War, henceforth fall outside their monopoly. The War of 1914–18, which replaces the universal of the bourgeois republican state by the universal principle of hostility among nations, is the prerequisite, certainly insufficient but necessary, for the phenomenon of

[12] Serguëi Tchakhotine, *Le viol des foules par la propagande politique*, Paris, Gallimard, 1939.

totalitarianism. As Furet strongly believes, it also enables a novel linkage between the passions – revolutionary and national. Italian fascism is born of this link; it is not a counter-revolution but a fully committed one which owes its success, above all, to its ability to appear as bearer of 'hope for millions of men' (XXS, 708).

This expansion of the subject effectively opens up new perspectives and enables one to envisage a separation between the revolutionary phenomenon and the hope of universal emancipation. If 1914–18 had not been the date of the passage from the revolutionary Left to the Right, in other words, from the emancipation of the human and social race to that of the nation perceived as a species[13], it accelerated it considerably and, above all, legitimized it. Since then, not only have revolutionary passions – national and nationalist – which will be discussed in the chapters on the subcontinent of India and Pakistan and the Middle East, stopped being exclusively European; moreover, a number of revolutions of the Left (for example in the cases of China and Algeria) have become, in fact, national, if not nationalist.

The contribution of the War to the transformation of the revolutionary phenomenon does not stop here. Indeed, more than the Franco-Prussian War of 1870-71 or the American War of Independence, that of 1914–18 was a scientific one, mobilizing large-scale technical proficiency (statistics, land-use, engineering, medicine). If the nation, in its 'vitalist' element and in its 'quest for survival' becomes inseparable from the military, the latter henceforth merges with science. Moreover, the War helped achieve in a certain sense the victory of the principle of scientific prophecy at the cost of traditional prophecies[14].

Till now, each belief system that aimed at interpreting evolution and thereby setting forward a road map for humanity, was shaped

[13] See Zeev Sternhell, *La droite révolutionnaire. Les origins françaises du fascisme: 1885–1914*, Paris, Le Seuil, 1984.

[14] Paul Bénichou, *Le temps des prophètes: Doctrine de l'âge romantique*, Paris, Gallimard, 1977, coll. "Nrf".

along highly speculative lines that made headlines during trial periods, within learned societies, friends' circles or perfunctorily amongst independent communities.

From now on, the science of the future becomes directly axiological, resulting in two consequences, opposed to each other but nevertheless with a close relation of dependence: it is either Social Darwinism postulating war for survival which is accepted as the ultimate end of the existence of the nations, or scientific predictability moving towards an immediate revolutionary promise through a teleological history. In fact, Furet, shows that the 'universal charm of October' was inseparable from the certitude of the existence of 'historic will'. 'Deprived of God', he adds, 'our time has divinised history as the advent of the liberated man. From this history, which has otherwise become a substitute for salvation, at least the reconciliation of Man with himself, the October Revolution was the mythological moment par excellence' (XXS, 593).

The war was 'democratique' in the sense that it originally mobilized the *demos* and was founded on the popular will, was also militarist, subjected to compulsions and hardships of War; it was testimony to organization skills serving as conditions for survival and axiology to achieve the realization of the 'historic will' advocated by Lenin in his famous tract, *What is to be Done*, that appeared in 1902.[15]

'Mirabeau or Robespierre did not know in 1787 that they were going to make the revolution. Lenin had all along known it' (XXS, 622) says Furet, as he had 'the idea of a science of history whose secrets were known only to an avant-garde. In his analysis, the War confirms it. The organizational 'technicality' which had so effectively replaced diplomacy during the War, is imperative in realizing a 'short–circuit history' (XXS, 596) instead of the

[15] For the complete text, refer to www.marxists.org/francais/lenin/works/1902/02/19020200.htm

opinion of transformation by reform or by evolution on which existed a social-democrat consensus.

Finally, against this bizarre backdrop of anguish, and at the same time of emancipation of passions and imaginations, one witnesses the emergence of another paradoxical combination of axiology and scientific-revolutionary messianism: what is promised by historical, teleological or eschatological certitude, requires intervention by a group, aware, ready to make sacrifices, but accepting the role of the *agent* of a plan which is external rather than that of the future of a society under construction. This capitulation facing the 'historic will' also determines revolutionary thoughts; henceforth it is not discussion, contradictory debate, which was for so long appreciated by the social-democratic tradition, or even speculative abstraction, but it is axiology which is going to determine the meaning of the words from 'State' to 'Revolution', from 'party' to 'class', from 'materialism' to 'revisionism'. Asceticism, the principle of militancy of all revolutionary battles, will also leave its imprint on thought, thus making it impossible to differentiate between slogans.[16]

Half a century after the Russian Revolution, political Islamism or Islamic Marxism will arrive through the works of the Egyptian Sayyed Qotb or the Iranian Ali Shariati at the same conclusion: the only ray of hope before man, legitimized as much by science as by eschatology, the revolution will not take place without a technique of seizure of power and without the agents who work for it. There will also come up a process fixing the meaning of the

[16] With regard to the Soviet political syntax, Furet refers to the surprise, deceptively naïve and of a rare 'pre-Orwellian' maturity of Boris Souvarine: "Not a fact, not a citation, not an idea, not an argument: impudent affirmations with half a dozen interchangeable words, coming from the 'top' (because even *that* is decided at the top level) Thus, in the phrase: "For the Bolshevik unity of the Leninist party", reverse the order of the adjectives, (and) you get 'For the Leninist unity of the Bolshevik party'; next reverse the order of the noun, you get 'For the Bolshevik party of Leninist unity' and so on. Is it not wonderful......' (XXS, 642).

words by axiology. In a few decades of dissent, terms as complex as *jihad* or *shaheed* will cease to be polysemic, no longer signifying that which the praxis would want them to.

DOES REVOLUTION LEAD TO A TOTALITARIAN SYSTEM?

A second line of enquiry that one can formulate, taking off from Furet's work concerns War, understood here as a continuation of revolution and a prerequisite for establishing a repressive, even totalitarian political order. It is known that in the three model revolutions, French, Russian and Iranian, war constitutes the second phase of the revolution to the point of becoming inseparable from it at least for a certain period. This deployment of revolutionary dynamics in the territory of large-scale violence and against the 'oppressed', recruited, willingly or otherwise forcibly, is in radical contrast with the universalist concept of revolution based on the fraternity of the human genre, of the oppressed classes or even of 'the community of the believers', in other words, that of the celebrated *umma*.

It is true that before adopting a belligerent posture without compromise, the three revolutions find themselves confronted with external attack with a view to destroying them leaving them no choice other than ensuring their stability through their transformation into a vast military apparatus. In all three cases, wars were led by popular forces whose determination was found to be iron-clad, rather than by military corporations, that had been largely dismantled by the revolution.

The link between revolution and war does not transform less radically its political meaning. Under a military order whose ultimate legitimacy rests on a *vitalist* register of survival and not on the universalist aspiration of emancipation, all resistance is perceived in terms of absolute enmity. The internal conflicts of the revolution, including the debates on its interpretation, are criminalized; political dissent against unlimited sovereignty by the 'people united' in defence of *its* revolution against external threat becomes an act of betrayal.

This militarization has major consequences on the final stage of the revolution and the formation of a coercive order, and a logical step forward. The war, in fact, marks the termination of revolutionary processes as a bearer of multiple and indeterminate possibilities; but it also radicalizes the revolution as a principle by sanctifying and condemning it for anchoring itself in the long term at the cost of the blood of its martyrs.

Putting an end to the war amounts to putting an end to the revolution. The discontinuities, the importance of which Frédéric Gros[17] reminds us, disappear, making room for an organic continuity between the external and the internal fronts, the civil and the military, commitment and technical organization. The war is the moment when the revolution propels itself to a presumption of innocence even though it is, in fact, in the process of losing it forever to transform into *power*.

As Furet says of the French Revolution, not only 'the Republic had no other powerful base other than War' (RF, 386), 'but by blackmailing the country with the threat of revolution, those in power seek, in fact, to justify, on the basis of an imaginary war, an augmentation of their prerogatives along with a curb on public liberty' (RF, 616). The Russian and Iranian Revolutions will find themselves in the same configuration: War will offer them a reason to toughen their stand, a context to defer promises, a cornerstone of power, an instutionalized means to blackmail on the home front, and naturally the opportunity to eliminate opposition groups, who were also the revolution's proponents.

Can one, for all that, establish a relationship between revolution, revolutionary war and totalitarianism? If such a link does exist, it comes from the order of probabilities and not from causality.

[17] Frédéric Gros, *États de violence: essai sur la fin de la guerre*, Paris, Gallimard, 2005.

One knows that Furet refuses to establish the slightest continuity, either in its specific context or in a long term, genealogical order, between the French Revolution and the totalitarian phenomenon of the 20th century. Certainly, he thinks that the Terror constitutes 'a repressive system organized by those at the top and institutionalized' and 'a system of government; or, better, an essential part of the revolutionary government. Its arm' (D, 158–159). But the totalitarian phenomenon goes well beyond the institutionalization of coercion by a committee to ensure its stability. To Furet, totalitarianism as a system, is infinitely more complex and is able to sustain a strong hope of deliverance, hope that it is nevertheless destroyed at the same time by its praxis (XXS, 115)[18]. It is not born of the revolutionary phenomenon as such, but rather of Europe at the end of 1914–18. Once again, the legacy of this war has the enabling effect of reassembling the necessary ingredients of ushering in a totalitarian regime: a 'hope' of the millenarist type, endowed, nevertheless, not only with scientific credibility, but certainly also a 'doctrine' which freezes as much the revolution as the knowledge of revolution, a 'strategy' of transformation of the political into the technical and a 'lust for power', quite openly. It is in a Europe, reconfigured by the War that the strange combination of monopolizing dictatorship *and* coercion of the State *and* revolutionary violence could come into being[19] and could promise salvation in the name of the state *and* in the name of revolution.

EGALITARIAN PASSIONS, THE NEW MAN AND REVOLUTION

The revolutionary challenge exposes the State as it shows that it is based on the principle of alienation which also regulates the

[18] Which certainly does not signify that Furet confines totalitarianism to this dimension alone.

[19] One will remember the surprise of Sebastian Haffner in the face of this strange combination. See his *Histoire d'un Allemand. Souvenirs 1914–33*, Arles, Actes Sud, 2002.

time. Whatever be its consequences in the long run, the revolution is first a jolt and a timely and axiological exit. Each and every revolution, including the Iranian, which, however, embodied in the elderly Ayatollah Khomeini, its symbol of resistance, is by definition youthful and recognizes that the *ancient* order had transformed the present into a rule of injustice and degeneration. Even after having served its time, the old order remains capable of unleashing oppression to prevent the advent of the time of justice and regeneration or at best to cultivate the illusion of harmony in order to endure the respite. In the final battle of 'Biblical' nature, as Michel Foucault would say, the young should not only "regenerate" society, but also provide it immunity from any further lapse. The revolution cannot set itself a more modest course, consisting simply of 'setting the record straight in the here and now'.

More than the absence of democracy whose meaning has undergone so much change in the last two centuries, it is the absence of justice and equality, read or perceived as such and always magnified by biased regimes which feed revolutionary passions. Not only are inequality and injustice, display of depravity in the dialectic of the master and the slave, synonymous with one another, they are also synonymous with alienation. We shall come back later to the place that Furet accords to the egalitarian passions, which do not only emanate from the oppressed or the victims of state exclusion. At present we shall limit ourselves to specifying that without being the sole causes, they partly explain the transformation of revolutionary *subjects* as individuals, subjected to a new coercive order born of the revolution.

Certainly, all constructions of power in a post-revolutionary situation imply the setting up of a short-term, reigning elite or of a *nomenclature*, and adopts a new order based, in its turn, on the alienation that the revolution wanted precisely to avert (from this point of view, the French Revolution is not an exception; XXS, 333). At the same time, however, all revolutions result in equalization of the conditions, often by those at the lower rung of society, at times in the form of gross exploitation to compensate for the slow growth in the technology of the labour force. There is nothing to indicate that this poverty was heartily accepted by the citizens of the egalitarian republic, born of the revolution.

One knows how much the 'revolutionary patience', Russian or Iranian, has rapidly given way to actual suffering and a mass indifference on the part of the population in relation to the rousing speeches of the two countries. It is nevertheless a fact that making grandiose plans made by and for the 'community', from the metro of Moscow to the monument of the martyrs in Teheran, helps heighten, rather than diminish the propensity of a revolution outside one's native country. The poverty, the price that the citizens have to equally pay to rightly attain equality, appears as evidence of the moral superiority of the revolution with relation to the capitalist system or *taghuti*, even as a mode of resistance to their worldwide domination. Thus, finding its explanation in this enemy from elsewhere, the injustice of poverty is not able to tarnish the justice of the regime, born of revolution.

There is quite a close causal link between the revolutionary egalitarianism of the subject and the equally revolutionary ideal, of the new man. The revolution is not only an exit strategy from alienation; by the expectations it generates and often the sacrifices it entails, it also becomes a project to equip society with necessary weapons so that it never feels tempted to go backwards. It does not only aim at reconstituting the 'united' family, discarding the unworthy 'father' and his lackeys from the 'castle', but also to radically reform the 'brothers' and 'sisters', transformed into citizens, on new foundations; shielding from corruption and egoism, sharing the same sufferings; the members of the new family know that the horizon of emancipation cannot be attained individually. This new identity necessitates a terrain where the revolution can show its superiority not only in relation to the former regime but also in the face of tyrannies threatening it, a terrain where there is commitment, sacrifice and prediction of the future. This place, as Furet points out, cannot be other than the cultural domain (T, LXX III).

THE REVOLUTION AND THE HATRED OF THE BOURGEOIS

Besides his work on the 20th century and on the French Revolution, *The Past of an Illusion* by François Furet enables us to understand the role of the 'hatred of the bourgeoisie' in the emergence and reproduction of revolutionary passions elsewhere; from Russia to Iran or from China to India, one can observe this hatred towards an aristocracy or even a ruling political class seen to be alienated from society. Emphasizing this fact undoubtedly constitutes one of the lines of cleavage separating Furet from the *apologues* of a liberal economic order.

To Furet, the modern bourgeois world is worn down by a hatred which is two-fold: the first being the hatred felt by the dominated, exploited, and excluded. (The latter are not terms used by Furet). The second, on the other hand, that the modern world has difficulty controlling, even more suppressing, emanates from within itself and is designated as the victim, if not of auto-destructive dynamics, then at least of radical dynamics. Indeed, they are as a matter of fact 'the children who have an intense dislike for the regime they were born into' and it is in their midst that the 'hatred for democracy becomes democratic' (XXS, 529, 532). We shall come back to the reasons inciting them to such hatred; continuing with Furet's arguments let us clarify that faced with 'authoritarian fathers', supported by their privileges, revolt becomes the only means for the young to achieve both their intergenerational rupture and their night of 4 August. It is only on condition of renouncing economic inequality of which they are the beneficiaries, that they are able to comply with, at least in imaginary terms, the equality promised by the 'nation' or society.

The egalitarian revolt, in which there is an active participation or involvement of the young generation – they are even found to give impetus to it – is the inevitable consequence of the contradictions between the promises of the state and its practices. 'Disinherited Man' – the bourgeoisie, in fact, is incapable of honouring the principles of equality that it advocates and waiving the privileges that he knows are unfair and petty.

Breaking another promise, it transforms into,

> ...traditionalist through fear: a negation of self that does not require a tradition. He hates the revolution that backs him up. Other than revolution, traditions belong to others – the monarchists, the aristocracy and these are like borrowed clothes. He relinquishes ancient titles, but he has none of his own. He has ceased to embody freedom and dons the mantle of the head of the family – tyrannical and authoritarian, with a mania for comfort and obsessed by property. In short, anything devised by the bourgeoisie backfires. His status raised through money, he can enter the inner ranks of the aristocrats; but this egalitarian tool changes him into a different kind of aristocrat, who is more bound to his riches than former aristocrats were to their origins. He applies the Rights of Man on the christening font but Freedom frightens him and Equality even more so. He has been the Father of Democracy. But democracy has uncovered how fragile governments are; at the same time the danger of numbers... of the poor. If the bourgeois was the 'Man of Renunciation', he is the 'Man of Untruth' (RF, 947–948).

Thus the bourgeoisie stops by blocking the horizon of its own universe and loses confidence in its capacity to govern it. Certainly, the rarity of revolutions proves that the State is able, as a general rule, to leave its mark in the long run; but even if Furet does not say it explicitly, in order to reach at that point, it (the state) has no hesitation at all to arm itself with economic liberalism, and sometimes simply to arm itself, against the demand for political liberalism which occasionally threatens it. The coups d'États of Latin America, just as the 'years of decline' in the 1970s are considerable events where the 'bourgeoisie' proceeds by anti-democratic means to ensure its survival. Still worse, as Pierre Hassner explains in a remarkable Seminar entitled *Conférence François Furet*, beyond the State, the bourgeoisie gives up even more completely its principles and becomes 'barbaric' to free itself from dealing with external threats[20], real or imaginary. But its conscience neither supports the repressive orders it imposes, nor, for that matter, the wars that it leads from outside and which are in complete contrast to its promises of universality, provoking new waves of internal protest. More than class struggle, though he emphasizes its importance, Furet draws our attention to another contradiction of class societies and the relations of domination and exclusion.

(THE) REVOLUTION AS CONFIGURATION AND RELIGIOUS AMBITION

With the promise of 'secular redemption' (RF, 812) that it fulfills within the state, the revolutionary act throws out a new challenge to the social sciences. It is true that the researcher can and should, like Tocqueville, Furet or Martin Malia, Theda Skocpol or Charles Tilly[21], analyse it as the consequence of a crisis rooted in this present world to comprehend it in terms of power and of relations between power, crises and struggle – social, political and economic. However, in this attempt, the event of a revolution can confront its own rhetoric on the exit from alienation, its proven eschatology, that consists of wiping the slate clean of the past (XXS, 594) and inventing a new time, of eternal justice. The researcher, then, will have no choice other

[20] Pierre Hassner, *La revanche des passions*, Paris, Société des amis de François Furet, 2004.

[21] Martin Malia, *Comprendre la revolution russe*, Paris, Le Seuil, 1980; Theda Skocpol, *States and Social Revolutions. A Comprehensive Analysis of France, Russia and China*, Cambridge, Cambridge University Press, 1979; Charles Tilly, *Les revolutions européennes*, Paris, Le Seuil, 1993.

than accept this discrepancy with his 'subject', but also as Furet does in his writings as a whole, and particularly in *The Past*, to restore its psychological and subjective dimension.

In a commentary on Tocqueville, Furet, in fact, insists on the contradiction between the state of being and the auto-representation of the French Revolution, a contradiction equally observed in the case of other revolutions, including the Iranian. 'What is so new about Revolution? Like some religious revolutions, it is supposed to be "universal", while it is social and political in nature' (T, XXIII). 'Choosing the regeneration of humanity as objective', he continues, "The French, towards the end of the 18th century wished to achieve in this world a kind of ambition which, according to the Christians, is fulfilled in the world beyond (T, XX, III)"'.

One can, in fact, hardly imagine a revolution not born of a revolutionary crisis, which is, first, a political crisis, then economic, cultural or even social. It is, however, evident, that a crisis does not offer instruments of its critical study with an internal reflexivity. As a complex process, it constitutes at first, an episode of doubt in relation to the established meanings of a given world. Paradoxically, but without contradiction with this statement of fact, it is also this condensed space-time during which a teleological study of the world becomes inevitable, the lines of fracture of the present being redrawn by 'the fascination of the verb [...and] the flow of eloquence' (O, XLIX) to be invested with a new meaning. Through this teleological invention, the present becomes the place of reinterpretation of the past and of self-projection in a collective being which never existed, still does not exist but already inhabits the future in its entirety. In this revolutionary heuristics, the historical landmarks of the past are viewed either as simple accidents on the way, marking the deviation from what the world was before its alienation (the state of nature, primitive communism or even the *asr-i-saada*) either from the events which stand witness to moments of repression or of resistance, testifying to the profound truth of the revolutionary teleology. Furet devotes a number of pages to the criticism of the philosophy of history (XXS, 302). A dangerous trap for the researcher, it, however, appears as the only support which enables a revolution to find a direction.

The revolutionary crisis signifies a loss of faith in the past, seen not only as the bearer of injustice and oppression but also corruption and degeneration. If all revolutions share a common deep rooted mistrust with regard to their existing present times, they are however, unable to maintain these relationships with the present age in the same manner. The French Revolution seems to be rapidly hurtling towards an aporia, insurmountable contradictions in reasoning for, as Michelet, who Furet cites, says: 'time did not exist any more, time had perished' (RF, 892). And, at least at first, 'instead of setting the time, the French Revolution speeds and splits it up. It is because it never succeeds in setting up institutions (RF, 877). It does not have 'any point of reference to the past or institutions in the present, a future, barely possible without delay and always distant' (RF, 878). True, after the 18th Brumaire, it will endow long lasting institutions, most of which still survive and establish an age that regulates the world, including its conflicts, which are shared by all; it is nevertheless a fact that for several decades, France will have lived in this fractured time space, also implying a break up in direction.

Inversely, right at the beginning, the Russian Revolution makes itself 'rigid' which also enables it to overcome the crisis of the 'decay of time'. The reason is that unlike its predecessor of 1789, it has a vanguard capable of taking action, and interpreting and determining at the same time the direction of its action. 'If the Bolshevik party is in charge of not only leading the revolution but also of predicting every moment its fate, all political disagreements within it, or within the International, are also a challenge to its foundation: its ability to lead class struggles according to the science of history' (XXS, 625). This organic rigidity not only leads to the formation of a classless society, if one glosses over the *nomenklatura*, but also to the subjection of the citizens to a time which is exceptional, regulated and loaded with an exclusive meaning. From this point of view, there is a distinct difference between the period of Terror during the French Revolution and the Leninist terror, and especially the Stalinist. The French Terror complies with an indeterminate trajectory which will end by removing its architects incapable of mastering the process set off by them; but since it is not a product of causal logic whose origins are in 1789, it ends by becoming a heavy historical digression, difficult to forget. Such is not the case with the Russian Revolution for which the opponents or those qualified as such by the authority, find themselves purely and simply relegated into something, timeless and spaceless, namely, the camps of Gulag.

THE REGIMES OF HOPE AND THE DESPAIR OF REVOLUTIONS

Furet insists, particularly in *The Past*, on the hope and also on the feeling of post-victory deception that revolutions give rise to. In the case of the French and the Russian, if not also of the Iranian, that he analyses, the success of the revolution spawns a process marked simultaneously by deception and a commitment to making sacrifices, by disenchantment and re-enchantment. If this fact is less visible in the long history of the French Revolution, it is no less present under the Constituent Assembly, the Terror or even Thermidor; players of the time have often taken recourse to the notion of betrayal to denounce the monopoly of the Revolution by a clique or by abandoning its objectives, defined differently by each of them (RF, 68). The 'betrayal' is, however, as much a fear or a plot, as it is hoped to be a revelation of the real meaning of the Revolution.

According to Jacques Pierre Brissot whom Furet cites on several occasions, 'I admit, gentlemen, that I have only one fear. It is that we would not be betrayed [...]. We need to have a lot of betrayals; there lies our salvation [...] the big treacheries will only be harmful to the traitors; they will be of use to the people (in general)' (30 December 1991; RF, 81). In Russia, for instance, the impressive *Cheka* of Vladimir Zarzoubrine[22], himself an outright apologist of the Terror and the Revolution, long before the advent of Stalin, acted as a machine for producing 'traitors', especially including within its own ranks. Qualified to be defectors to join the opposing camp of class struggle, they (as well as their families) are considered as a biological threat to the Revolution. Finally, in Iran, the Revolution divided its supporters into two camps: the 'traitors', executed or exiled, and the faithful. The internal moratorium on the meaning of the revolution which *had prevailed* after the death of Khomeini in 1989, was for a long time suspended without, however, preventing the return to the categories classifying the traitors and friends from 2005 under President Mahmoud Ahmedenedjad.

The power born out of the Revolution is not, however, the only one to initiate such types of qualification and disqualification. The revolutionaries of 1917 experience, after the death of Lenin, the fear of a Thermidor that they redefine as a counter-revolution or diverting the revolution to benefit a conspiracy, therefore, a betrayal. This historic trauma, going back to the 'mother revolution', prevents the old Bolsheviks from grasping the unfinished nature of their revolution, as well as the true nature of the Stalinist dictatorship. During the Iranian Revolution of 1979, to which we shall return in the chapter of this book devoted to the Middle East, the issue of betrayal soon appears, as early as 1980. The radical, even the liberal Left, without taking into account some members of the clergy, accuses Khomeinism of having a stranglehold on the revolution which distorts its meaning; the Thermidorian hypothesis is widely evoked (sometimes even ardently desired) after the death of Khomeini in 1989. There is

[22] Vladimir Zarzoubrine, *Le Tchékiste*, Paris, C. Bourgeois, 1990.

also a fear or inversely, the expectation of a Thermidor stemmed from the lack of understanding of the hitherto novel nature of the Iranian Revolution and its ideology, socially conservative but potentially messianic, that was in other words, Khomeinism.

In a way each and every revolution, before long, falls prey to a betrayal, because it is forced to, institutionalize and get acquainted with the 'establishment of power'; to use categories used by Sorel or Tilly, this leads to a passage from revolutionary violence to force and the coercive power of the state and also from utopia to ideology, in the sense in which Mannheim uses the term[23]. It also becomes tied up with a situation hitherto unknown, namely the sanctity of power. If under the former regime (as from time immemorial, for that matter), 'Power' wished to sanctify itself by the distance it had created with its subjects, the revolution had changed the rules and introduced the duty of direct sacrificial intervention as a condition of citizenship in the political arena. Furet clarifies, while speaking on the French Revolution, that 'each individual can, henceforth, take over the old divine monopoly, that of creating the human world, aiming at recreating it' (D, 168). The shutting down of the revolutionary process does not only imply suppression of freedom of speech of the majority, but at the same time introduces a huge gulf between the rulers, sanctified in the name of a cause, and the ruled; a distance that no symbol can illustrate better than the famous wall of the Kremlin.

The institutionalization of the revolution does not signify simply putting an end to the movement which is at its base; it also implies indoctrination of the anti-establishment forces into a coercive body, organized and mobilized by the authorities. The power, born of the revolution, develops a double legitimacy by the monopoly of revolutionary sacrifice which gave birth to it and

[23] George Sorel, *Refléxions sur la violence*, Paris, Quartier Libre, 2006; Charles Tilly, *The Politics of Collective Violence*, Cambridge-London, Cambridge University Press, 2003; Karl Mannheim, *Idéologie et utopie*, Paris, Éditions de la MSH, 2006.

by bringing out its only authorized work. This double integration transforms it, whether willingly or not, into a power, corresponding to the model of Carl Schmitt; it makes another appearance with unlimited sovereign powers, to point out friends and traitors; it raises novice revolutionaries, as worthy adversaries and uses a symbolic violence against them, which precedes, accompanies and legitimizes post-facto the use of physical coercion.

The post revolutionary mobilization, in fact, enables transformation of the revolutionary dynamics into a force, always mobilized and at the same time spearheads the fulfillment of miracles (revolutionary wars in France, industrialization of the Soviet Union, fierce resistance of Iran against Iraq with the support of the USSR, Europe and the United States). The price to be paid is postponement of the ideal of liberty and equality to devote (oneself) to the sacrificial reconstruction and protection of 'the homeland in ruins', and always 'in danger'. The sanctification of the revolution and its icons – whether they are its founding father, its martyrs, its Committee or its Party – gives birth to an integrated symbolic whole, enclosed within itself in the sense that each symbol is derived from a whole and encompasses the whole, whose (very) mention itself forbids dissension. As Glassan Salamé says in the Arab context, 'to leave', synonym of *Khurudj* consequently becomes a betrayal.[24]

If institutionalization of a model revolution takes place in its native homeland, the evolution of the regime of hope and despair that it gives birth to, works out elsewhere among the supporters in other countries, proceeding with time towards a sanctification from a distance. After being tarnished in its own country it makes way for submission either through fear or out of habit, a revolution may continue to thrive in another country under a

[24] Ghassan Salamé, "Ou sont donc les démocrates", *in* Gh.Salamé (ed.), *Démocraties sans démocrates. Politiques d'ouverture dans le monde arabe et islamique*, Paris, Fayard, 1994, p. 23.

new magical spell and even endure, depending on particular cases. In this 'elsewhere', where the geometry is variable, a great many are those who fight to join the ranks of the universal liberator of revolution, in order to lessen, by their sacrificial actions, the sufferings of the revolutionary country and thus to accelerate the end 'of the tyrants' who make their repressive global order live on. Thus, under the combined effect of action of 'the homeland of revolution' and genuine desires, processes of revolutionary re-enchantment take place.

As Furet shows in the case of the Russian Revolution, these processes, however, give rise to as much deception, over the years, as downright dissidence. In that case, an impossible equation then comes up in the style of Hirschman[25]. It is about positioning oneself in relation to the revolution according to the three choices which present themselves: *Exit, Voice* or *Loyalty*. 'What is to be done', indeed, from the time it is known that 'the rot has already set in', that there is 'something rotten' in the land of revolution, of liberty, of the proletariat or even of the *umma*? 'What is to be done' if one arrives at the conclusion that those in power have betrayed the revolutionary cause or adopted bureaucratic frameworks by imposing, along the way, a security apparatus, far more cynical and repressive than that of the former regime?

The trajectory of the tragic heroes of European communism, presented by Furet and then taken up again in a remarkable novel by Antonio Munoz Molina[26] (Nicolas Lazarevitch, Pierre Monatte, Pierre Pascal, Victor Serge, Boris Souvarine, Charles Rappoport, Albert Treint and many others) shows that the response to this question is infinitely heartbreaking. True, one can attempt and simply 'exit' from the challenge but after years of militancy and sacrifice, this solution is painful as it boils down to 'capitulation';

[25] Alfred O. Hirschman, *Défection et prise de parole: théorie et application*, Paris, Fayard, 2005.

[26] Antonio Muñoz Molina, *Séfarade*, Paris, Le Seuil, 2003.

and as a result a betrayal and move to the 'enemy camp'. On the other hand, one can be anchored in the lexicon of the inimitable which continues to point the finger at the 'big enemy', be it imperialism or the *dar-ul-harb*. With a heavy heart, also through an excess of zeal, one continues to follow the 'birthplace of (the) revolution'. One produces a rhetoric of justification that transfers the responsibility of the aberrations of the revolution to its enemies or invokes attenuating circumstances always external to the revolution, which dampens its dynamics without modifying its end. Thus, the people responsible for Stalinist terror or for the Agreements between the USSR and Nazi Germany, or that of (the) mass executions of the left militants in Iran in the 1980s, 'simple episodes not at all affecting the ultimate end of the revolution', would put the onus not only on the 'homeland of the revolution' but on 'Anglo-French imperialism' or the 'Great Satan'.

Two other options may equally appear, in varying degrees, to ensure a coherence between the continuity of past struggles, then the rupture, even of producing added radicalism in (the) commitment. The former consists of reviving an internal critique of the system which enables one to come out of the revolutionary Church, while continuing all along with a dialogue in a 'common language' with the misguided 'faithful', starting with those who exercise power in the 'homeland of the revolution'. The passage from Leninism-Stalinism to anarchism, Trotskyism, and in a certain sense, Eurocommunism in the 1970s, and in the case of the Iranian revolution, from Khomeinism to a Quotobism or to a much less mystic Shariati, represents the 'noble exit path' enabling one to regain autonomy with regard to the model, to evoke another discursive and partisan legitimacy, an *authentic* tradition without, however, 'going over to the enemy'. The best option that we observe, more particularly in the attitude with regard to the USSR during the years 1970–80, consists of coming out of the system by a deeper radicalization, blurring the contradictions, that prohibit a debate on the past. Maoism of the 1970s, no doubt, partly owed its success to its capacity to shield the past from all kinds of interrogation by changing the register and the scale of promises within the communist circle.

REVOLUTION: A PASSION IN DEMOCRATIC SOCIETIES AND...ELSEWHERE

To Furet, revolution is passion, sustained partly by the demand for equality and liberty, and partly by the doubt, melancholy and anxieties of modern times. In Furet's usage, this term finds its origins particularly in the work of Benjamin Constant and not in the theories of modernity of the Habermasian type; it defines the bourgeois state (XXS, 518), constantly weakened by the dynamics of challenge that it generates. Therefore, revolutionary expectation whose intensity changes depending on the periods, generations, players, social classes and the regime of subjectivity of each period, does not constitute an aberration of modern times but its very nature. At the extreme opposite of Francis Fukuyama who, along with Samuel Huntington, left a mark on the intellectual debates at the turn of the 1990s, Furet believes that the end of the Soviet system would not be synonymous with the final victory of bourgeois democracy and that its future remains uncertain.

> History again becomes this obscure tunnel where man enters into obscurity without knowing where his actions will lead him to, uncertain of his destiny, deprived of the illusory security of a science he makes so much of. At the end of the century, deprived of God the democratic individual sees the Goddess history shake at its foundation: it is a fear that he has to handle (XXS, 1075).
>
> No one knows yet, he continues, whether our democratic societies are going to live, deprived of political messianism or whether they are going to make other monuments, witness to inexhaustible egalitarian hopes (XXS, 935).

What does one say, then, about the rest of the world where armed protests from the Islamists to the Maoists, continue to be so real ?

In fact, Furet does not say much about it. His world is limited to France and the United States,[27] two revolutionary countries which were his own, in varying degrees, and then the former Soviet Union, the 'homeland' of his first commitment, and finally East Europe. Apart from a brilliant interpretation of *Islam and Capitalism* by Maxime Rodinson (XXS, 307–310) and a few lines on Algeria (Post-French, concerning therefore the bourgeois state,[28] including the disappointments it has had), his connection with the Middle East is limited to the interest he has in Israel, a country he admires and views critically. But is Israel actually a part of the Middle East? According to him, Israel is at the same time the fruit of universal Europe in the sense that it is modern and bourgeois, and excluded even from this universal by the anti-semitist violence caused by it (See his texts, XXS 260–300).

Furet's silence on the non-bourgeois world largely explains the choice of this volume to make one look beyond Europe which, whether one wishes it or not, has occupied a central place in the history and the imagination of the world for two centuries. Convinced, as much by Europe as by their own course of Westernization of not having any history, a number of intellectuals across the world looked towards the old Continent in the hope of being a part of its universal, in other words, the only universal, helping to build the future it had promised. This is a culture which, as its intellectuals and prophets had advocated, must be marked

[27] Let us here, however, keep in mind that Furet who maintained a complex relationship with the United States was undoubtedly one of the rare observers to grasp its dynamics of radicality. His fascination for this country goes hand in hand with the numerous criticisms on its present state and his insistence on the need for a vigilant democracy so far as (its) future is concerned. (See, among others particularly XXS, 249 and the following one.)

[28] "Wherever Left intellectuals had made its universal values available, it encountered a national and religious conscience; while looking for the Bolshevik party of 1917, it found Islam, Boumediene in place of Lenin" (A, 39).

by the advent of the Revolution. As the history of westernization of the rest of the world is not only that of the determination to change the civilization, predicted by a thousand and one thinkers, dictators or reformers, one of them being Mustafa Kemal of Turkey, it also consists of coming to terms with the West till the end, that is, including its destructive and/or revolutionary passions and promises. In this sense, as Nichanian, in his detailed study on Armenia[29] says, the success of 'Marxism-Leninism' elsewhere in the world comes especially from the fact that it constituted the last Western avatar.

However, on the other hand, in the course of the 19th and 20th centuries, a certain West could equally take a look at the East to take refuge. Two examples as proof: while Kemalist Turkey disowned its past, so clearly influenced by the 'Asiatic darkness', there were a number of those in Europe, who looked towards this 'spiritual East', in the search for sources of regeneration of the West.[30] And whereas Maoism in China made a moral order reign that even the most integrationist of Christians or Muslims would have found repressive, the European youth of 1968 invented sexual freedom by brandishing photographs of Mao.

Spiritual or scientific, revolutionary or non-axiologic, would the universal be the mirror for our first imagination and hopes? The following articles will try to make an attempt to answer these questions.

CITED TEXTS OF FRANÇOIS FURET

A: *L'atelier de l'histoire*, Paris, Flammarion, 1982.

D: François Furet et Mona Ozouf (eds.), *Dictionnaire critique de la Révolution française*, Paris, Flammarion, 1988.

[29] See the trilogy, *Entre l'art et le témoignage. Littérature arménienne du XX siècle*, Paris, Metis Press, 2006–2008.

[30] Dorothée Guillemarre-Acet, *L'Allemagne, l'Empire ottoman et la Turquie républicaine: relations politiques et liens culturels (1908–1933)*. Doctoral thesis of l'INALCO, prepared under the supervision of François Georgeon, 2006.

H: "Préface", *in* Élie Halévy, *Correspondance, 1891–1937*, Paris, Fallois, 1996.

O: (avec Ran Halévy), "Préface", *Orateurs de la Révolution française*, vol. 1: *Les constituants*, Paris, Gallimard, 1989.

RF: *La Révolution française*, Paris, Gallimard, 2007.

T: (avec Françoise Mélonio), "Préface", *in* A.de Tocqueville, *Œuvres*, Paris, Gallimard, 2004, coll."Nrf", vol.3.

XXS: *Penser le xx siècle*, Paris, Robert Laffont, 2007.

Fidel Castro enters Havana, Jan 8, 1959

Source: https://en.wikipedia.org/wiki/Fidel_Castro

Daniel Ortega becomes President of Nicaragua, 1985

Source: https://es.wikipedia.org/wiki/Daniel_Ortega

chapter 2

Two Revolutions—Cuba 1959 and Nicaragua 1979:

From the War against Tyranny to Totalitarian Dictatorship

Gilles Bataillon

CUBA AND NICARAGUA

Few revolutions have aroused as much hope as the ones that took place in Cuba and Nicaragua. The former takes place just at the opportune moment immediately after the Krushchev question and bringing Poland and Hungary into line. It gives revolution back its glow. It brings to an end the tyrannical and corrupt regime of Batista. It brings to power leaders in whom international public opinion wishes to see models of integrity incarnating a new idea of revolution.

The seizure of power by Castro and the movement of 26 July are perceived as factors that set the masses of the Third World going; 'a peasant revolution', according to Sartre led by the intelligentsia. The face of this revolution is primarily that of Castro, who put to an end all kinds of social injustice, and remodeled the country under the leadership of a National Institute of Agrarian Reform (NIAR), formed of cadres belonging to the Rebel Army. Twenty years later, the Sandinista revolution is welcomed with no less fervour by world public opinion. While hopes, pinned on the socialist experiences of South East Asia, end abruptly with the rise of the totalitarian dictatorship forged by the Khmer Rouge and the flight of thousands of Vietnamese boat people towards Thailand, the revolution of 19 July 1979 offers the opportunity of a pluralist revolution.

Guerillas of the Sandinista Front of National Liberation (FSLN), men coming from a bourgeois rank, long opposed to Somoza, launch a programme of moderate reforms without anyone appearing to impose his own hegemony. Even better, the revolution of 19 July gains from the benevolence of the Church. Its clergy supported the armed struggle against Somoza, celebrated a *Te deum* to mark the national reconciliation just after the fall of Anastasio Somoza, and several priests become part of the government. The government announces a policy of non-alignment and respect for human rights. These two revolutions have, each in its own way, reintroduced the idea that tyranny could be defeated by armed struggle without even forging for all that a new bureaucratic power structure that hangs over society. If both these revolutions aroused the enthusiasm of the progressive Left, they appeared at the same time to be at odds with the world of 'real socialism', represented by the Soviet Union or China. They are credited, at least at their initial stage, with the ability to associate aspirations with social equality with the concern for liberty or even, for the latter, to combine Christian and Marxist aspirations. The two revolutions, one after the other, appeared as so many new experiences, auguring new possibilities of emancipation for Third World countries. The paths traversed by these two revolutions very soon created tensions and oppositions within, and gave rise to passionate debates in the world of public opinion.

It is during the first few months of their victory over the previous regimes that cracks appear within the anti-Batista and anti-Somoza coalitions and differences crop up in their two revolutions. Between six months to a year, the consensus against the overthrown tyrants unravel completely. In Cuba as in Nicaragua, there is a resurgence of totalitarian powers which emerge quite easily at the expense of other elements of the opposition which had similarly taken part in the overthrow of the tyrannical regimes. Six months after the fall of Batista, Castro imposes his hegemony and that of his followers in the interim government. Urrutia, the interim president, whom he had nevertheless helped to get appointed, is replaced by an ardent supporter of Fidel Castro, as are his other supporters – ministers anxious to maintain a balance among the different powers and the multiple constituents of the anti-Batista revolution.

Moreover, Castro imparts a radically new style to existing Cuban politics. Those opposed to the modalities of revolutionary justice, the agrarian reform launched in May 1959, and the reorganization of the armed forces, are stigmatized like so many traitors endangering the stability of the nation. And these denunciations take place in people's rallies, broadcast by most of the radio stations and shown on television channels where the protestors are required to acclaim the decisions of Castro or his close supporters. All attempts to oppose his views are denounced as plots against the revolution.

December 1959 witnesses the first political trial against members of the Rebel Army (RA) who (voluntarily) choose to renounce their responsibilities to protest against the course taken by the revolution. Accused of betrayal, they are condemned to long-term imprisonment at the end of a long trial where they are made to play at the same time, though without success, the roles of both the accused and the prosecutors against themselves. In January 1960, freedom of the press and freedom of the trade unions are suppressed. Relations with the United States become strained and remain so without a break and in March 1960, while the Cuban government refuses the last offers of American co-operation, Eisenhower gives the green signal for the CIA to train up anti-Castro exiles.

In May, the Cubans establish diplomatic relations with the USSR. In retaliation, the United States refuses to buy the remaining quota of Cuban sugar for 1960, while the USSR retorts by putting in a bid for it. In August, the United States passes a resolution at the Organization of American States condemning Cuba. In October the Cubans nationalize the big companies – their own as well as foreign. The United States declares an embargo on trade relations before severing diplomatic relations with this country in January 1961. At the same time, the first underground counter-revolutionaries organize themselves in the island; in April, troops of exiled Cubans, backed by the United States, land at Playa Giron and are battered by the Cuban army. In December, Castro declares while giving a speech on the formation in future of a unified communist party: 'I am Marxist-Leninist and I will remain so till the end of my life'.

Similar ruptures are seen in Nicaragua as well. From the first month of the revolution, the Sandinistas start imposing their hegemony on their rival associates. They take possession of the installations of the former journal of Somoza which should have been used to start an official journal of the Junta Government of National Reconstruction (JGRN) to launch there the daily of the FSLN, *Barricada*. They put pressure on the independent unions so that they integrate the Sandinista Union of the Workers (CST) and persecute very brutally those who refuse to join them, particularly those close to the journal *El Pueblo*. They entrust the responsibility of the new army to one of their people, and again manipulate the composition of the cabinet of ministers for their profit. In mid-April, they instruct the non-Sandinista members of the JGRN, Violeta Chamorro and Alfonso Robelo, that the provisional legislative power, where the FSLN did not have the majority, to induct new members, those who would enable them to gain a majority. Their dismissals and public protestation of one of them, Alfonso Robelo, in return, lead to the deployment of an accusatory rhetoric which compares from now on, each and every opposition to the decisions of the Sandistas, to a connivance with the former Somoza regime.

The first anniversary of the revolution on the occasion of which there was a rally, gives the Sandinistas an opportunity to announce that the elections are not a priority for the revolution besides imposing censorship on the press. In October 1980, Jorge Salazar, President of the Council of Private Companies, who attempts to hatch a plot with officers of the new Sandinista army, is shot down by the police. A month later, Robelo and his supporters are not only the subject of press campaigns but the target of Sandinista militant attacks and their rallies are banned for their collusion as 'the foreign aggression'.

At the same time, the relationship with the Church becomes more and more strained with each passing day. Similarly, relations with the United States are going to deteriorate slowly. In February 1981, the Americans who had not appreciated the refusal of the Nicaraguans to condemn the Soviet invasion in Afghanistan (January 1980), protest against the support to the guerilla offensive in El Salvador (January 1981), and suspend their economic aid to the country. Furthermore, it is from the end of 1979 that peasant groups who had backed the FSLN, that is, the MILPAS (anti-Somoza popular militia) reorganize in 1980 to protest the agrarian policy of the government.

In 1981, the leaders of the underground, peasant resistance movement become more important, while the first clashes between the Indian *miskitus* and the Sandinistas break out. Following these clashes a section of the *miskitus** activists go into exile, planning to embark on an armed action. Beginning in 1982, the different anti-Sandinista armed groups, formed in the interior of the country, come in contact with the supporters of Somoza who were in exile. They form the *Contra* and undertake the first of the armed operations backed by the United States. After having forcibly displaced the Indian population living in the border of Honduras, the JGRN proclaims a state of emergency

* The Miskito are a Native American ethnic group in Central America. Editor.

and suspends fundamental rights. The country goes into a new civil war, *Sandinistas versus Contras* (1982–87), which will go through a brief period of lull during the elections of 1984 that the Front will win.[1]

How do we view these dramatic changes since the first year of these revolutions, in Cuba in 1959 and in Nicaragua from 1979 to 1980? By what means did these two revolutions that ended undeniable tyrannical regimes, and then instituted new totalitarian powers? Three major interpretations of these transformations have been put forward. The first rightly emphasizes the influence of Latin American political culture and within this, the dominant role played by the system of *Caudillismo**. Castro's ability to play the pre-eminent role since the fall of Batista, including entry to Havana – all stem from this heritage. As Hugh Thomas[2] very subtly remarks, he is not only a 'Caribbean Bonaparte' but also 'a resurrection of the apostle Marti '**. In fact, he is immediately going to do away with the revolutionary process and supplant all possible rivals. Keen observers of the Cuban experience will underline this ability of Castro to draw on this style as well as on that of populism. From this period, the inevitable downward spiral into the institution of a totalitarian system emerges, away from its Latin American cultural heritage roots.

[1] The best account of the beginning of the Sandinista revolution is the one by Shirley Christian, *Nicaragua Revolution in the Family*, New York, Random House, 1985.

[2] Hugh Thomas, *Cuba, The Pursuit of Freedom*, New York, Harper and Row, 1971. Except other explicit references, I would borrow all my facts and figures on the Cuban revolutionary process from this work, and especially from the following portions: Book 9, "Victory: the lyrical illusion", pp. 1037–92 and Book 11, "The Clash: 1959–1962", pp. 1193–1422.

* Caudillismo, a system of political-social domination, based on the leadership of a strongman, that arose after the wars of independence from Spain in 19th-century Latin America. Editor.

**Refers to Jose Julian Marti Perez, Cuban author, poet and national hero. Editor.

Castro would be a sort of Cuban Peron, a radicalized Peron. The Cuban bureaucracy and its systems of privileges, very early brought to light by an observer, as scrupulous as René Dumont, turned to the same heritage as Caudillism.[3]

The Nicaraguan author Sergio Ramerez and other eminent members of the Sandinista reform movement like Sofia Montenegro or Giaconda Belli, or even a former Sandinista like Moises Hassan Morales, made similar statements about on the downhill road taken by the Sandinista revolution.[4] Caudillism, which has been the common link of the political practices of Nicaragua from the 19th to the 20th century, weighed heavily on the revolutionary experience. A good number of the nine members of the National Directorate of the Sandinista Front of National Liberation (FSLN) were cast in the same mould. They connived to exclude all rivals so that they could lead the revolution; this resembled the way previous conservative and liberal heads of State had carried out agreements in order to rule over the country.[5] Some members of the Directorate of the Front had moreover considered, as (did) their conservative and liberal predecessors, that politics should be a source of personal enrichment[6], from where comes the phenomenon of the *piñata.*

[3] *Cuba est-il socialiste?* Paris, Le Seuil, 1970. See also his earlier book, *Cuba. Socialisme et développement,* Paris, Le Seuil, 1964.

[4] Sergio Ramirez, *Adios Muchachos.Una memoria de la revolucion sandinista*, Mexico, Aguilar, 1999 and Silvia Cherem, *Una vida por la palabra..Entrevista con Sergio Ramirez*, Mexico, Fondo de Cultura Economica, 2004; Sofia Montenegro, "Es revolucionario el FSLN?" and "La "Herotica" national"; Giaconda Belli, *El Pais bajo de mi piel*, New York, Vintage Books, 2002; Moisés Hassan Morales, *La maldicion del Güeguense*, Managua, 2009.

[5] In this connection we shall refer to the book of Xiomara Avendano Rojas, *Elecciones Indirectas y Disputa de Poder en Nicaragua: el lento camino hacia la modernidad*, Managua, Grupo editorial Lea, 2007.

[6] I shall go back to this point in my study "De Sandino aux *contras*. Formes et pratiques de la guerre au Nicaragua", *Annales*, 60e année, n 3, mai–juin 2005, pp. 653–88"; see also the book of Moisés Hassan Morales, op.cit.

A second explanation focuses on the central role of American intervention. Faced with the intransigence and blindness of the United States, one can understand why Castro and the Sandinistas would feel the need to bolster national sovereignty. So these revolutionary leaders did not have solutions other than to turn to the Soviet bloc to act as a counterbalance to American imperialist interference, which led to their inevitable alignment with the former.[7] Castro, like the Sandinistas, had a rational choice, choice of a certain inevitable path, because of the international context. Thus, to continue with this line of interpretation, the first dissensions within the anti-Batista or anti-Somoza coalitions would not have been able to come into being, had it not been for the pressure of foreign influences, primarily North American. Such was the case in Cuba at the time of the initial opposition to Castro, within the Rebel Army (RA) or the Movement of 26 July (M 26/7), that is, of Urrutia – the provisional president imposed by Castro – and other politicians. The fissures within the anti-Somoza bloc would develop in the same way in Nicaragua twenty years later. Alfonso Robelo and his followers, businessmen of the COSEP (Higher Council of Private Enterprises) and the Catholic Church would, in the same way, follow foreign injunctions. Everybody would act in liaison with North American pressure groups, whether from the world of business, or from the world of politics and military, or in liaison with Costa Rica and Venezuela.

The final mode of explanation puts emphasis on the adhesion to the communist model which was established since the coming of Fidel Castro as well as the Sandinista leaders. The former had,

[7] It is the theory that prevailed in progressive European circles in Latin America or in the United States and today in the circle of those who believe in alternative globalization. This thesis goes back to a certain development of (ideas of) Trotsky on the encirclement of the revolution and its importance in its bureaucratization to transpose them to the Cuban and Nicaraguan revolutions. Claude Julien and the team of the *Monde Diplomatique*, of which he was the first director, were great propagators of this vision carried on through different media.

as early as 1959, the intention to create a regime after the Soviet model and the latter wanted to follow Cuba. According to Ted Szulc, a long time journalist with the *New York Times*, Castro had secret alliances, since the first weeks of the revolution, with the 'old communists' of the popular Socialist Party and who had since then started a socialist revolution, in liaison with the Soviet emissaries.[8] In his Memoirs, Hubert Matos, one of the first to oppose Castro, makes more or less the same observation.[9] Castro straightway refuses any idea of collective leadership within the revolution and comes to rely more and more on those close to the communists. And it is from the month of March that the armed forces are infiltrated by the pro-communists, mostly selected by Guevara and Raul Castro, or those who were loyal to them. Taking the case of Nicaragua, without necessarily describing the manner in which the Sandinistas made their viewpoints prevail over those of their rival associates in the battle against Somoza, Jorge Alaniz Panel[10] who was earlier close to the Sandinistas and was the first to publish a very remarkable eyewitness account of the revolution, has shown how the FSLN had never put a stop to their plan of building a socialist society. Analysing meticulously and taking into account the different texts emanating from the Front as well as the actions of their leaders, he demonstrates how the process of modernization practised by the FSLN in 1978–79 was purely a façade. His thesis 'Analysis of the Circumstances and the Tasks of the Sandinista revolution', where the NL (National leadership) reminds one that the political objectives of the Front are to

[8] *Fidel a Critical Portrait*, New York, William Morrow and Company, 1986; French translation: *Castro, trente ans de pouvoir absolu*, Paris, Payot, 1987, "Quatrième partie la revolution (1959–63)", pp. 401–533.

[9] *Como llego la Noche*, Barcelone, Tusquets, 2002; French translation: *Et la nuit est tombé*, Paris, Les Belles Lettres, 2006. We shall refer particularly to chapters 29, "The revolution in progress", and 30, "The communist conspiracy", pp. 322–63.

[10] *Nicaragua, una revolucion reaccionaria*, Panama, Kosmos-Editorial S.A., 1985.

establish its hegemony and bring about a 'definitive liberation' in the country – is very solidly backed by a capital document distributed among the cadres of the FSLN a few days after the victory over Somoza. The authors of this document outline a programme of action which aims at subordination of all the rival politicians in the FSLN or eliminating them and nationalizing the economic sector at the head of which the Sandinista cadres, the backbone of the new country[11], ought to be placed. The latter interpretation is often supplemented by another which sees in the infatuation, the object of which was as much the radicalization operated by Castro, as the process of 'hegemonization' of the Sandinistas, the sign of an adhesion to the egalitarian model of a classless society.

These different interpretations bring to light the factual elements crucial to a clear understanding of these revolutionary processes; thus they suggest so many ways of understanding the reversals which took place within the span of a few months in these two revolutions. It is on the basis of these interpretations that I would like to attempt an analysis of these changes which constitute the emergence of a totalitarian power in various forms, both in Cuba and in Nicaragua. It is indeed important to leave aside, even if temporarily, the basis of an argument conducive to guiding a more systematic research on the coming to power of totalitarianism. Rather than opposing these different interpretations, one against the other, I would link them in order to understand how these two regimes which came to power with a gap of twenty years, first in Cuba, then in Nicaragua, are, to repeat the words of Claude Lefort, 'the product of an extraordinary condensation of a heterogenous process which coexisted in the same space and at the same time'.[12]

[11] Known under the name of 'Document of the 72 hours', this text has been published as Annexure to the book of Octavio and Elvyra Sanabria, *Nicaragua, Diagnostico de una traicion. El Frente Sandinista de Liberacion Naional en el poder*, Barcelona, Plaza & Janes Editores, 1986.

[12] *La complication*, Paris, Fayard, 1999.

Indeed, the whole question is that of understanding how the appearance of landmarks and new practices takes off from the breeding ground of traditional forms of power which are going to be radically remodified. There is absolutely no doubt that it is this anchorage in adherence to past habits which is going to give all their force to these new modalities of social organization. It would be advisable to again go back to the socio-political contexts in which these two revolutions take place. What is significant about the reversals of Batista and Somoza? Is it the eviction of the unpopular tyrants and a readjustment of the political game in practice till then, or on the contrary, do these reversals combine with a longing for inventing a new political model and radically question the existing social order?

What to say then of the response encountered by Castro and those close to him and that encountered by the Sandinistas? Where and how do they differ and break new ground by their programmes and by their contact with the popular masses and their rival allies in their fight against Batista or Somoza? When and how will this specificity be imposed and why will their rivals be ousted?

ORDER AND VIOLENCE

Like the other Latin American countries, Cuba and Nicaragua have been, since their independence, in search of a stable political order, and this, amidst great uncertainties. As Daniel Pécaut has very rightly noted, 'the uncertainty […] is about the identity of the people and the formation of the nation-state, as if the one and the other remained in suspense'.[13] This is to say that the Cubans and the Nicaraguans harboured recurring doubts about social unity. Thus, neither the faith in the Free Market nor the theory of general

[13] *L'ordre et la violence, evolution socio-politique de la Colombie entre 1930 et 1953*, Paris, Éditions de l'EHESS, 1987; see pp. 9–15.

sovereignty is sufficient to give a proper foundation to society. Quite on the contrary, reigns the idea that society, left to itself, is destined to fail to achieve success and to lapse into barbarism. Without doubt the forms of their interrogation vary from Cuba to Nicaragua, but the belief that society not controlled by 'those at the top' is destined to chaos, lingers. The counterpart of this doubt is, at the highest point, evident in the role handed down to the state, which is perceived as the instrument par excellence of society.

These depictions are linked to a conception of politics where order and violence occupy central positions and are complementary. The action of the state and the socio-political actors is part of a world, in many respects, non-democratic. Without doubt, the liberal-democratic legitimacy constitutes a horizon which none think of crossing[14], but this reference goes hand in hand with practices and representations which have largely broken away from certain crucial moments of the democratic experience. Thus the conflict is not at all recognized as legitimate, no more than the social division is perceived as insurmountable other than in the symbolic order. Quite on the contrary, the state, together with the socio-political actors, intends to intervene to put an end to social disorganization. Violence concerns the modalities of actions of the protagonists taken together. It also goes back to what constitutes a 'margin' of the civilization, of the urban or the rural working classes, the Blacks and the Indians. This is to say that it does not constitute a functional reverse side of the order but that these two categories have their foundation in the same vision of the society as primarily incomplete and, hence, condemned to barbarism, if it is not put in order 'by someone at the top.'

This feeling of an incomplete society seems particularly strong in Cuba. What does one think of the conditions of independence,

[14] On this point refer to the reflections of Octavio Paz, "America latina y la democracia", *Tiempo nublade*, Barcelona, Seix Barral, 1983; French translation: "Latin America and democracy", in *Une planète pour quatre ou cinq mondes*, Paris, Gallimard, 1985, coll. "Folio-essais."

of the role played by the USA, of the Platt amendment limiting the sovereignty of the emergent nation? The strength of the nation appears to be the least problematic. The importance of single crop cultivation of sugarcane in the economy of the island, for example, does not speak in favour of social regulation by the laws of the market. Indeed, the development of the sugarcane economy resulted in a boom in the 1920s – 'the dance of the millions' – was followed by a collapse just after 1929, which brought about the ruin of numerous producers. This gives rise to a double thematic in the Cuban political rhetoric – that of decadence and that of a necessary reawakening of the new elites.

This sentiment of incompleteness is no less present in Nicaragua all along the 19th and at the beginning of the 20th century. The Nicaraguans never had the impression that they belonged to a nation. On the contrary, they are a fascinating part of a system included in subcultures – the liberals of Leon and the conservatives of Granada – not only rivals but often openly at war with each other. In addition, the sovereignty of the country was demolished by the interventions carried out by the United States at the beginning of the century (1912–25, 1926–33). Here too these doubts about the integrity of the nation instill desires of regeneration of the society filled with neo-Thomist images.[15] Seen from these situations, one cannot miss the parallels between Fulgenico Batista and Anastazio Somoza Garcia. The success of one as of the other is due to their ability to appear throughout the time as architects of a social order. Adoption of social legislation will enable both the former and the latter to integrate the subaltern classes, and then, to appear as civilizers of the social groups, dismissed till then as barbaric. These same laws outline the principle of a necessary complementarity of capital and work in as much as they curb the appetite of the oligarchs. Also, they are the ones to put an

[15] The writings of José Coronel Urtecho and those of Pablo Antonio Cuadra best illustrate this project.

end to the armed confrontations between rival entities and force them to compromise. Another common metaphor of the Cuban and Nicaraguan political imagination is that of social corruption and of its necessary regeneration – a metaphor which becomes all the more important at the end of the regime of Batista and that of the latter of the Somozas. In this respect, it would be proper to systematically compare the discourses and the rhetorics of Chibas in Cuba with those of Pedro Joaquin Chamorro of Nicaragua. It is, indeed, important to try to understand how both of them reutilize Christian principles for rebuilding a society free of corruption, and how these schemes are reutilized by Castro and the Sandinistas to legitimize their respective enterprises.[16]

THE GAME OF POWER STRUGGLE

The seizure of power by Castro and the Sandinistas not only took place in the contexts where democratic forms were, to a great extent, absent; but it was also a direct continuation of political practices, extreme polar opposites of the democratic system. As Charles W. Anderson[17] shows, this policy is perceived by the Cubans as by the Nicaraguans as a mechanism of manipulation and negotiation of power among competitors; their resources serving as the object of reciprocal evaluation in order to reach an accord negotiated at the top. This process of evaluation of the claims of different protagonists takes place by demonstrations of force where violence plays a central role. Thus, the Cuban as well as the Nicaraguan politics had, as backdrop, armed confrontations

[16] I have studied the process in the Nicaraguan context in *Genèses des guerres internes en Amérique central (1960–83)*, Paris, Les Belles Lettres, 2003.

[17] See *Political and Economical Change in Latin America*, Princeton, D.Van Nostrand Company Inc, 1967; Spanish translation: *Cambio Politico y Economico en la America Latina*, Mexico Fondo de Cultura economica, 1974. For views of this author see also François Bourricaud, 'Dictadura, dictablanda et la question de l'hégémonie en Amérique du sud', in Léo Hamon, *La fin des dictatures*, Paris, Economica, 1983.

followed by arrangements at the top among the heads of rival entities. These practices are accompanied by an implicit agreement so that 'this system of power struggle' could accommodate new protagonists if they were able to give proof of their power so much so that the new entrants had to demonstrate by their actions that they had a nuisance value contingent upon consideration of some of their demands. As a result, there is frequent recourse to violence – from demonstrations to skirmishes, to attacks on property – less against the people and never against the most prominent figures of the military top brass. In the same way, appealing for foreign aid or material resources, with diplomatic support, and even armed men, is never found to be illegitimate, quite on the contrary. The rules of the game demand, on the other hand, that none of the rival associates are to be eliminated from the circle of those struggling for power, even if their resources are found to be depleted, and that too, drastically. The only case where this implicit rule may be transgressed is when one of the contenders tries to prevent the entry of newcomers in the long-term or wants to monopolize power solely for his profit. Another phenomenon must be emphasized in turn that counters to some extent the argument of the political base of power struggles. The Church remains, on the other side of its separation with the state, the key to the vault of social order. That is to say that religion and politics are not separated, but intertwined and that the omnipresence of that which Claude Lefort calls 'theological-politics'[18] cannot be analysed as the simple sign of a political function of the religious.

In this regard, the modalities of access to power by Castro and the Sandinistas borrow from the rules of the game followed by the power rivals. The former is looked upon as a newcomer on the scene of rivalry for power and he organizes multiple forceful demonstrations to make himself known and admitted into the inner circle. The attack on the Moncada barracks (1953) is, indeed, a

[18] See 'Permanence du théologico-politique?', in *Essais sur le politique XIX–XX siècles*, Paris, Lc Scuil, 1986.

maiden move, where Castro poses as the reincarnation of Marti[19]; but this is also no less a demonstration of force which comes in the middle of a multitude of others carried out by the members of different small revolutionary groups challenging the coup d'État of 1952 which made Batista head of State for the second time.[20]

Subsequently, when Castro had landed with his companions, after facing significant obstacles, according to Granma* (1959), they find themselves competing with other urban resistance groups such as the Federation of Revolutionary Students and the Revolutionary Directorate. The first Manifesto of the Sierra is completely in line with the power system of rival groups and calls for the installation of a government containing all opposition forces.

The demand for Batista's deposition and the refusal to come to a compromise with him is because he appears as symbolizing a corruption henceforth found to be intolerable by a large number of Cubans. The trajectory of the Sandinistas is, in many respects, parallel to that of Fidel Castro; Castro, though straightaway, speaks the language of those in the race for power. The Sandinistas will, all along the 60s, and a major part of the 70s, refuse this, only to rally around him in 1978.

But, since then, and till the beginning of the 80s, they (the Sandinistas) will only be using this language. Indeed, since the assassination of Pedro Joaquin Chamorro in January 1978, the Opposition, coming up from the ranks of the conservative clan to the last of the Somozas, multiplies the demonstrations and the strikes against the person who it accuses of being behind the crime. And it is through this game of rivalry in the demonstration of force that an agreement is going to take place among the

[19] Let us remember that Marti is the hero of Cuban independence who all Cuban politicians refer to.

[20] On this point we shall refer to Theodore Draper's article "Le Castrisme", in *De Marx à Mao Tsé Toung*, Paris, Calmann-Lévy, 1967.

* Granma – the daily newspaper of the revolutionary government, established in 1959, following the outcry against Batista. Editor

Sandinistas, the Church and the 'bourgeois' opposition which will lead to the formation of a junta government of national reconstruction, making room for the contenders of power with the notable exception of Somoza and his followers.

Once in a prominent position in the new circle of those aspiring for power, Castro and the Sandinistas are going to speak a language unknown to the Cubans and the Nicaraguans, that of conflict between those for the people and the Enemies of the people, that of formation of the new man, or even that of abolition of all distinctions between Power, Right and State. But here too, it should again be underlined that the Cuban leader, like his Nicaraguan counterparts forges the new by transforming the old elements. The discourse on the rebuilding of the world, the necessity of regeneration of society borrow each time a good number of their elements from Christian symbolism. Guerillas, who descend from the Sierra Maestro and march triumphantly towards Havana claim to be Catholics. Moreover, the Church will celebrate the fall of Batista. As for Nicaragua, the revolution straightaway claims to be Christian. Just after the assassination of Pedro Joaquin Chamorro in January 1978, the Archbishop of Managua – Miguel Obando – justified through multiple Biblical parables, the recourse to armed struggle against Somoza. The victory of the Opposition is celebrated as a resurrection. The Archbishop and the prelates will receive an oath from the members of the Junta government of national reconstruction, before giving them their benediction and before celebrating a *Te Deum*.

FROM POPULISM TO THE POWER OF THE EGOCRAT[21]

If Castroism and Sandinism both became established as totalitarian forms, and are cast in the same revival mould that follows the

[21] The word 'egocrat', coined by Solzhenytsin, denotes Stalin and the cult of which he was the object in *The Gulag Archipelago*. The term and its use by

syntax adopted by the power contenders, Castroism will partly borrow from the repertory of populism, while Sandinism will adhere to the system itself.

In 1959, a series of moves taken by Fidel Castro and his followers, such as the creation of special tribunals against 'war criminals', the personal intervention of Castro during the trial of the aviators* to obtain their death sentence, the fight against the autonomy of the universities and the independence of the student organizations, the creation of the National Institute of Agrarian Reform (NIAR), making the trade unions as well as the press toe the line, are evidence of imposition of a totalitarian order. These instances are an affirmation of an omniscient power, incarnating a society free from all contradictions, and for which all forms of 'otherness' are considered in terms of 'the antagonism between the people as One and the enemy of the people' in the words of Claude Lefort (Lefort, 2005). Also manifest is the idea that a Power incarnated by a Commander-in-Chief whose authority renders null and void all distinctions between Right and Power, Knowledge and Power, and Capital and Work. What should be noted here is how almost none of the players are in a position to signal this symbolic change which is linked with the ascent of power of a new form of domination.

Thus, before May, 1960, the Church did not have words to condemn publicly certain actions of the new government. At best it solicited clemency for some particular death sentences very discreetly without ever questioning the basis of the restoration of capital punishment by the new government or without criticizing the holding of special tribunals. This difficulty of the Cubans to

---

Solzhenytsin have been analysed at length by Claude Lefort in *Un homme en trop,* Paris, Le Seuil, 1976.

* Some pilots belonging to Batista's army were accused of bombing the civilian population, and later found innocent of charges brought against them in court. Furious at this decision, Castro ordered the reopening of the case and the pilots were found guilty and condemned to death. Editor.

grasp the distinctive feature of power established by Castro comes from the fact that his actions are a part of what Daniel Pécaut has called 'populist configuration',[22] even if it is to be liberated from it. Indeed, the politics of agrarian reform, announced since the beginning of January 1959, and implemented a few months later, much like the wish to control the syndicates, is a typical populist experience. One intends to put an end to the social conflict and go back to a possible and sudden appearance of barbarism, which is triple-faced: that of conflict itself, that of indecent yearnings for the oligarchy and, finally, that of immaturity of those at the subaltern level – workers or landless peasants. The foundation of the National Institute of Agrarian Reform and subordination of the trade unions to the state, are some of the ways of putting an end to antagonisms, of creating a bond where the State is the master. Appeal for humanism of the revolution, of exaltation of 'Cubanity', the triumphant march from Sierra to Havana, the rallies where Castro delivers his first marathon addresses in front of the most composite audience, are regarded as ways to signify equality of the Cubans beyond differences of class and status. Such an equality among people taking part in these demonstrations does not form a community of equals, capable of creating horizontal social bonds, but a totality which owes its existence to the ability of its chief to attract large numbers of people and to organize this into a holistic plan of action by the authority at the top.

The individual is a kind of civilizing hero leading a barbarian mass who reappropriates for itself the qualities of its leader. Likewise, the willingness of the revolution to mete out punishment to war criminals is, at the same time, a way to show an insurmountable social division between the followers of Batista and the revolutionaries and to affirm the wish to reunify it (the society) by the execution of those responsible for creating division. This division between people, between the victim and the torturer

[22] Op.cit, pp. 245–54.

who belongs to a minority, obviously has something of a myth reminding one of the division between oligarchs who have all, and the people – *descamizados, decalzos*, who have nothing.

There is a fundamental difference between Castroism and populism. The former, far from being taken in the perpetual oscillation of seconds, and also liberating themselves from the 'impossible', have reduced the actual (not imaginary) gap between the social and the political, and have succeeded in bringing about stable institutions. Thus, the setting up of new social relations, *via* putting into effect agrarian reform and the subordination of trade unions, enables it to erode the power of former social actors, whether they concern oligarchies or popular organizations which populism has never succeeded to reach out to. Quite, on the contrary, the former merely went from one compromise to another.

Here, with Castroism, these actors are eliminated or reshuffled. Furthermore, the state is no longer at a distance from the different social actors; there is a fusion forming a new entity dominated by an 'egocrat'. The fantasy is no longer that of a lost community that must be restored. One is on the opposite side faced with the creation of a new world, and in a certain way, a really new world. And if Castro's communism follows in many ways the past of Cuban populism, it is important to note how it is radically different from it, projecting something as real which, till then, remained in the realm of imagination, thereby undergoing a long term transformation which was originally only ephemeral.

FROM THE SYSTEM OF POWER STRUGGLE TO THE SANDINISTA STATE PARTY

It is just after the victory against Somoza that the Sandinistas are going to revoke the past agreements with the other constituents of the Opposition. This willingness of the Front to impose its 'hegemony on the revolution' creates an image hitherto unknown in the Nicaraguan political practices, that of *first among equals*, within the circle of the rival contenders for power. The Front thus obtains the dismissal of Bernardino Larrios – an ex-officer of the National Guard – opposed to Somoza – and his replacement at the head of the armed forces by one of his top ranking leaders, Humberto Ortega. In parallel, the FSLN nominates men who were totally devoted, into the new judicial apparatus. In December 1979, a cabinet reshuffle confirms the increasing importance of Sandinism in the political scene. The minister of planning, as those of agriculture and industry who were all bourgeois, 'opposed' to Somoza, are dismissed and replaced by the Sandinistas. These changes at the top are accompanied by the setting up of multiple mass organizations, the Sandinista Committee of Defence (SDD), the Organization of Women (AMNLAE) or of the Sandinista Youth (SY), trade unions, each of which is a vertical relay of power of the Sandinista Front. Whatever be the reservations which gave rise to these changes and innovations, among the different currents of anti-Somozist opposition, they are never directly opposed to them. Quite on the contrary, far from calling for the creation of an independent judicial power and a body of bureaucratically – organized functionaries, or even demanding the convocation of general elections, the associates opposed to the Sandinistas mobilize their forces to try in the same way to get a foothold in the new state apparatus or to establish a network of influence capable of thwarting the actions of the FSLN. Likewise, when the Sandinistas rely on the support of the Cubans to create a new army and a new police, or to adopt certain directives of agrarian reform, their rivals – conservatives and Christian Democrats – multiply their picketing near the embassies of North America, Panama and Venezuela to try to influence the policies of the JGRN. That is to say, all the players of the Nicaraguan political scene share the same political vision where demonstrations of force and its use are considered as legitimate political resources.

What is more, certain sections of the Church, as a good number of large conservative families, an entrepreneurial milieu and the editorial staff of the *Prensa* view quite favorably measures taken against the sectors which are extreme Left. Thus, not only the hostile attack on the takeover of the independent Marxists-Leninists of the journal *El Pueblo*, those aimed at the trade unions which do not intend to pledge allegiance to the new central Sandinista, but also the public humiliation suffered by some of their leaders, are accepted as gestures, normal and at the same time salutary. The Sandinistas appear as an entity likely to train and civilize the subaltern classes somewhat like Anastasio Somoza Garcia had done in the 1930s and 1940s. And if Alfonso Robelo, one of the members of the Junta Government of National Reconstruction (JGNR), denounces the willingness of the Sandinistas to 'concentrate all power in their hands' and resigns from his post as a mark of protest, the majority of the socio-political players are not at all disturbed by such talk. Above all, they perceive the opportunity of occupying the place earlier taken by Robelo in the game of an alliance with the Sandinistas. As a consequence, the Sandinistas will not have any difficulty in finding his successor. And it will be the same just after the resignation of Violeta Chamorro. We shall thus see the leader of MISURASATA, a native American-Indian organization on the Atlantic coast, making the most of this opportunity to try to win more seats in the State Council which holds the provisional legislative power.

That is to say that even before publicly announcing that it was against the principles of the system of power struggle among rival groups, the Sandinista Front could establish the foundations of an unprecedented authority in Nicaraguan society. It is not merely a party well established in the state apparatus and in complete control of its new repressive system, bringing at the same time under its control the judicial, executive and legislative powers: it is a new body altogether making its appearance in society. It is not just a new contender for power; it is also an entity that its rival associates have put in charge of civilizing, a kind of Nicaraguan 'barbarism', embodied as much in the Indians in the Atlantic Coast as in the working class urban youth or in the landless peasants. Therefore, when, during the takeover of power and the establishment of JGRN, the Sandinista and the national colours were solemnized in the same manner, the Church and the multiple rival associates of the Front – not only gave credence to the idea that the Sandinistas were *primus inter pares* and some kind of *senior pars* in this new Christian city of post-Somozist Nicaragua. Moreover, they made a hole that swallowed up the FSLN and challenged the moral authority of the Church as the last resort, and its power to differentiate between civilization and barbarism, ultimately its power to achieve social cohesion.

But for all that one cannot minimize the rupture introduced by the FSLN in October 1980, when it declares itself the 'avant-garde conscience of the country'. By making this announcement the Front frees itself from all rules emphasizing the impossibility of expelling a contender from the circle of rival associates – be it that of stifling his freedom of speech, or it that of preventing an attempt on the life of the top leaders of rival bodies. The kind of publicity given to the two murders committed by the state just before and just after this declaration is particularly illustrative. On 17 September 1980, the day Somoza was assassinated in Paraguay, the Sandinistas, instead of claiming any responsibility for this murder, though they were very much behind it, declare it 'the day of national joy'. The headlines in the *Barricada* simply read: 'public condemnation, Somoza Dehayle has been executed, he has paid.' – and releases a communiqué – from the National Directorate – reminding readers of the 'genocides' committed by the dictator. The comment on this 'execution' has a tone that sounds very Biblical: 'One who has lived by the sword shall perish by the sword'.

Just after the death of the President – Jorge Salazar – which took place on 17 November during an assassination attempt fomented by the police, the tone is quite different. If the Home

Ministry exonerates the Police of the General Directorate for State Security from the murder declaring that the death was caused by an exchange of fire at the initiative of Jorge Salazar with those who came to arrest him, Thomas Borge and others, holding high positions in the police, justify the turn taken by this 'arrest'. They however, maintain that the President of the COSEP was a traitor who has been plotting against the regime. Thus, without claiming directly to have the power of life or death on those who they consider counter-revolutionaries, the Sandinistas do not hesitate to declare that henceforth they not only have all the powers to simultaneously draw the line between legitimate criticism and betrayal within the circle of their rival associates but also that their opponents have no solution other than complying with, without any resistance, all the orders of the police. And, armed with this new power they claimed for themselves, the Sandinistas will, from now on, assert themselves as a new body symbolizing the revolution and rejecting any opposition as a kind of resurgent Somozist barbarism.

SOCIAL EQUALITY AND THE BUREAUCRATIZATION OF SOCIETY

One would be mistaken if one considers these transformations only as political or ideological. They are linked to social changes which have far-reaching effects on the Cuban and Nicaraguan societies.

The Cuban government is going to take up a series of measures which would be of immediate benefit to the working classes. Decrees are issued to reduce not only the lowest rent by more than 50%, but also that of electricity and telephone charges. Properties of former Batistiens are confiscated and from 1 March, Castro starts giving away land to the peasants. These initial measures are soon followed by decrees to plan an agrarian reform and create the National Institute of Agrarian Reform (NIAR), a new state apparatus completely under the command of the leader of the revolution. This new body not only has the power to confiscate properties worth more than 400 hectares, but even more to entirely reorganize the country. It is divided into 28 zones, each placed under an administrator of the NIAR having a free hand in charge of the departments of public works, urbanization, housing, education policy and health.

As Antonio Annino[23] has very intelligently put it, emphasizing that organizing agrarian reform and the considerable power bestowed on the NIAR mark the victory of the members of the RA (Rebel Army), namely, men from Sierre, extremely loyal to Castro. It was a victory over the urban militants of M26/7, known as men from (the) Llano (from the plains) who were considered to be fiercely independent. The NIAR is not only an instrument of power loyal and subjugated to Castro; it is an apparatus which is also going to reform the society by confiscating and redistributing private property and the means of production. At the same time it enables the formation of a new class of men who acquire another identity thanks to their participation in this body of technocrats entrusted with the responsibility of reforming the country. This new organ supplants, to some extent, the Rebel Army (RA), some of whose members, such as, Hubert Matos, were important and influential and could make use of their revolutionary past and their experience as fighters, questioning or challenging certain decisions of Castro. The NIAR is going to wipe the slate clean by welcoming, on equal terms, men whose only qualification was to have been identified by Castro as loyal revolutionaries. And there will be many to compete in order to occupy these new posts: whether they are members of the Popular Socialist Party, Castro's companions

[23] Antonio Annino, "La réforme agraire et le communism à Cuba", *Communisme*, n 85–86, Paris, L'Âge d'Homme, 2006, pp. 65–83 and *Dall'insurrezione al regime. Politiche massa e strzategie istituzionali a Cuba 1953–1965*, Milan, Franco Angeli Editore, 1984.

of struggle or simply opportunists, all eager to be a part of the new power and of its emoluments.

One finds a very similar logic in Nicaragua. The Government issues, all along the first year of the revolution, different orders in favour of the working classes: lowering of the rent in urban areas by 40% to 50% (in December 1979), lowering of the rent price of arable (agricultural) land (January 1980), and fixing the maximum price of a number of food items. This regulation of prices is followed by a policy of confiscation and nationalization. The exile and escape of the supporters of Somoza would enable confiscation of a quarter of the arable land, most of which is going to be administered by the National Institute of Agrarian Reform, formed in October 1980. At the same time, the insurance companies and mines are nationalized. These nationalizations, implemented at the initiative of the new authorities of the State, are accompanied by multiple effective confiscations of movable and immovable property as well as of land in the rural areas. This process of expropriation, which sometimes takes the form of pure and simple looting, particularly at the expense of those who were suspected of being Somozists, is such that in November, the JGRN forbids the civil and military authorities from confiscating movable and immovable properties and that in March, compensations are paid to the rural landlords who had suffered forcible expropriation. These nationalizations which took place at the initiative of the highest authority of the state, like confiscations, carried out little by little, depending on the relationship with local forces in the different urban zones or in the countryside, to which is added a particularly important external aid, are going to bring about unprecedented social transformations.

The new powers, as much on the national as on the local level, were thus in possession of very important resources and this in a country whose administrative apparatus, linked with the former regime, was either abolished, such as, the police and the courts; or disrupted – a large number of government officials and employees are exiled – or have just formed an organization like the NIAR. The movement for confiscation of power by those at the top, carried out by the Sandinistas, is going to come with a real bureaucratization by those at the lower rung, organized at the initiative of the Director of the Front and also by the first Sandinista militants, entrusted with the highest responsibilities and searching for someone to rely upon. The Sandinista Defence Committee, the new Police and the Army, the NIAR, are thus going to offer positions to all who were on their payroll but were, for a long time, without any political responsibility. If many are women or men who are mobilized to support the revolution, there are others, especially within the SDC, who are, above everything else, opportunists preoccupied with building their career. And, finally, some are former supporters of Somoza, mostly looking for ways to make up for their past misdeeds and are ready to make exaggerated ideological promises in order to succeed in doing so.[24]

It is impossible to fathom the dynamics of these two revolutions if one does not take into account these phenomena of bureaucratization by the functionaries belonging to the higher rungs, confiscation of power by Castro, his supporters and the Sandinistas and these forms of bureaucratization by those belonging to the lower rung, multiplication of all kinds of revolutionary committees, forming new administrative apparatus or renewal of those already in place. It would also be right to analyse jointly the following: the emerging thematic of 'the new man', the central role given to the state and the practical and effective government. We know that certain beliefs led to obvious economic blunders and the attempt to wipe the slate clean of the former 'habitus', and resulted in ignoring elementary accounting rules in cooperatives or production units.

[24] On this point we will refer to the books, already cited, by Jorge Alaniz Pinell and Moisés Hassan Morales.

René Dumont makes very sensible observations on the manner in which the agrarian reforms are carried out both in Cuba and in Nicaragua, twenty years later.[25] The eyewitness accounts of Hubert Matos, and those of Carlos Franqui[26] or K.S. Karol[27] on Cuba, of Jorge Alaniz Pinell and Moisés Hassan Morales as former sympathizers of the Sandinistas about Nicaragua, are important statements about certain blunders in economic matters. All this emphasizes to what extent these shortcomings, lack of regard for experience, faith in self-proclaimed experts or those known according to their acquiescence to the wishes and whims of those who have just come to power, were present from the first months of these revolutions. One must also compare the different 'revolutionary' concepts of culture, particularly visible in the literary campaigns, especially in Nicaragua. All and sundry, children and adults alike, got an opportunity to learn, to read and write and acquire some kind of a new autonomy; they were now better informed and were able to voice their opinion without any constraint. This (process of) learning is at the same time a real revolutionary one, like catechism, which places the Sandinista Front and its galaxy of heroes over-hanging Nicaraguan society.

The Sandinistas, from Sandino to Carlos Fonseca Amador[28] and the nine members appointed to the National Directorate of the FSLN, are all at the same time not only the *de facto* power: they also represent a new centre bringing together knowledge – technical, political or juridical – to political power. Here then is the first matrix of experience of totalitarian power, visible in slogans such as ' The DN orders...' or other such statements that oppose Castro.

But this is not merely, as Hannah Arendt has remarked, denying the value of experience that leads to injustices one has seen against

[25] René Dumont, op.cit., and *Finis les lendemains qui chantent*, Paris, Le Seuil, 1983.

[26] Carlos Franqui, *Retrato de familia con Fidel*, Barcelone, Seix Barral, 1981.

[27] Kewes S. Karol, *Les guérilleros au pouvoir*, Paris, Robert Laffont, 1970.

[28] The founder of FSLN.

agronomists and economists or teachers and intellectuals who call for other methods and denounce some particularly glaring economic failures.

This new political-intellectual conformism is truly an ideology – in the sense in which Marx uses this term – deceptive, serving a new social class, in this case, the bureaucracy.[29] Indeed, this ideology, this justification of a power without precedent is also that of new relations of production and forcible appropriation. It is of little importance that the bureaucrats are not proprietors through the means of production like some movable or immovable properties; also it does not matter that their total salary is little different from that of the most modest government officials. In fact, they have access to a number of privileges: confiscated houses or apartments to live in, transport, exclusive shops, and permission to import consumer goods from abroad without having to pay any duty. There is no doubt that a new social pyramid is recreated: it goes hand in hand with the expropriation of a section of the former wealthy classes and their fall in status does not, in any way, amount to a general equalization of the conditions of life.

One observes, quite on the contrary, in Cuba as well as in Nicaragua, the emergence of a new privileged caste that owes their position and the accompanying benefits more to their political conformism than to their talents measured in terms of a general universal usefulness. One also witnesses cases of favouritism and misappropriation of public funds which are not codified by law or which even openly contravene the legalities, but they exist none the less. It is, therefore, impossible to see in the call for state control and confiscations, as in certain policies, inevitably putting down the role of the moving force of the new revolutionary states and their administrations,

[29] I shall obviously refer to the great book of Marx and Engels on the subject: *The German Ideology* and also to the remark of Claude Lefort in 'Outline of genesis of ideology in modern society' in *Les forms de l'histoire*, Paris, Gallimard, 1978.

simple operations of rhetorical overstatement; essentially, these are speeches and practices favouring a new social class: the bureaucracy. Its role is not only glorified intellectually, it is also granted innumerable privileges.

This cursory glance at the first year of these two revolutions does not, in any way, claim to conclude interrogations; rather it opens up avenues for deeper, more serious investigations as much on the questions of the types of political sociability *in force and in use*, in Cuba in the fifties and in Nicaragua in the seventies. How did these *habitus*, to borrow the term used by Mauss, shape the political practices of the revolutionary players, once allies in their fight against the former regimes, but simultaneously rivals when they assert their superiority at the expense of their competitors? How have hierarchical *habitus*, where order and violence occupy a central position helped the emergence of totalitarian practices and has particularly encouraged the reincorporation of Knowledge and Right in the role of Power? It would be proper to analyse in great detail how the vocabulary of anti-Americanism and the past practices of a very short-sighted imperialism of interference of the United States, could be utilized by Castro and the Sandinistas alike to establish and justify the installation of totalitarian powers, even though the United States was, earlier, benevolent with regard to these two revolutions. Finally, it is important to take up afresh the study of these two revolutions in terms of 'total social fact' to borrow another expression from Marcel Mauss. How does the advent of totalitarian powers touch at the same time the political field – the central role of the parties, ideological – faith in the new man, but also economic and social – the advent of the bureaucracies and of a peasantry, integrated with the state? All these studies, if they attempt to describe and compare the phenomena, country by country, institution by institution, must be concerned with the effects of resonance among the political, cultural, economic and social arenas.

GLOSSARY

Rebel Army (RA): guerilla led by Castro since his return to Cuba in December 1956.

Barricade: daily of the FSLN, established in July 1979, following the outcry against Somoza.

Sandinista Central of the Workers (SCW): trade union under the FSLN, established in July 1979, following the victory against Somoza.

Contra: abbreviation of Counterrevolution, an expression used by the Sandinistas to denote at random different armed organizations which appeared in 1981, aiming to fight the FSLN.

Sandinista Front of National Liberation (FSLN): first established in 1961 under the name Front of National Liberation by Carlos Fonseca Amador, in 1964 this guerilla group takes the name of the Sandinista Front of National Liberation.

El Pueblo: Nicaraguan Maoist journal.

Movement of 26 July: movement launched by Fidel Castro during the attack on the Moncada barracks on 26 July 1953.

Piñata: name given to the properties that the Sandinista appropriated after their electoral defeat in 1990.

Shia cleric, Ayatollah Khomeini

Source: https://en.wikipedia.org/wiki/Iranian_Revolution

chapter 3

The Ups and Downs of Revolutionary Passions of the Middle East

Hamit Bozarslan

It was all in the recent past and yet it appears to have already faded into the distance that the Western world remained terrorized by the Middle East, not because it was Islamic, still less, because it was Islamist, but because it constituted a radical territory for the 'wretched of the earth' with strong Left leanings. Serving as a reference for the revolutionary passions and imaginations across the world, it is inspired, in its turn, by an 'elsewhere'; a varied geometry, stretching from South Asia to Latin America.

Before going into further details let us take the example of Leyla Khaled which serves to illustrate our point. Born in 1944 in Haïfa, this Palestinian, who posterity will remember as a member of a commando responsible for the hijacking of four aircraft in 1969, had this to say thus explained the reasons that made her so deeply committed:

> Che lived and died like a hero. And I, a 'revolutionary', have been living in the tranquility of far away Kuwait, while my people desperately needed a revolutionary and a hero of the calibre of Che. I decided to rejoin the ranks of the revolution[...]. I would make bombs with the atoms of my body and build a new Palestine with the fibres of my soul.[1]

[1] For the text, see Jean-Paul Charney, *Principes de stratégie arabe*, Paris, l'Herne, 2003. p. 292.

For this young militant, the passage to revolutionary violence was a response as much to the laxity of the Bolivian peasants who had abandoned 'Che' to his fate, as to the Arab regimes, the Conservatives as well as the Left, who had abandoned Palestine to confront its own destiny all by itself.[2]

Unlike the earlier generations of committed intellectuals, Leyla Khaled was not inspired by a positive model, an idea or even by a prophecy, providing the key to make the present intelligible and to look farther into the future. The world, as it appeared to her, could no longer be reformed by scholarly political leaders or by massive projects of modernization; it could only be liberated by being committed to sacrifice. Strengthened by the cause and the lifeless body of 'Che' – this symbol became almost Palestinian- Khaled broke from the particular and took up the cause of the world of suffering and oppressed classes of people in general. Acceptance of the heritage of 'Che' as a revolutionary inheritance radically modified the conditions of her entry into the realm of the 'universal'; henceforth, her horizon of liberation meant martyrdom and sacrifice. The 'median' point of a long quest, turning from Westernization to Islamism, to which the 20th century was a witness, the 'Khaled-Che' episode thus acquired a heuristic value, helping to understand the ups and downs, the good and the bad phases of the revolutionary passions in the Middle East.

PERIODS OF REVOLUTION IN THE MIDDLE EAST

According to Bernard Lewis, the Ottomans had neither grasped the radicalism of 1789 nor, for that matter, the symbolic impact of the execution of Louis XVI, so similar to the regicides – certainly exceptional but hardly novel – that they were familiar with in their own history. On the other hand, they were deeply scandalized by

[2] Ibid., pp. 534–38.

the denial of God during the Revolution.[3] More than a century later, while a number of Ottoman intellectuals openly declared themselves atheists, the term *Revolution* had become, the Turk thinker Cemil Meriç tells us, 'the most terrible word in our language: plotting, revolt, weakness of the State – were the signs of this evil disorder. The only word which could express the anarchy in Turkey was: revolution'.[4]

At the turn of the 20th century, the spectre of revolution was hovering over the two banks of Bosphorus. An impressive number of communities, comprising the Christian population, defined the Empire as the Kingdom of Darkness in Asia and were searching for the future in national emancipation, even in socialism. Furthermore, the Muslim civil and military intelligentsia, formed at the expense of tremendous sacrifices for serving the State, had itself become the importer of European revolutionary ideas. Much like the Khadjaras in neighbouring Persia, the reforms undertaken by the Ottomans in order to assure the survival of the two states, had triggered off processes that neither of them was able to bring under control. A thousand year old political culture, quick to detect behind each discord the spectre of the *fitna* was shattered, while the words *inqilab* and *ihtilal,* with multiple meanings but denoting, in the latter instance, revolution, appeared everywhere. Yet the jurists tried hard to keep intact the political doctrine of Islam – formed between 10th and 13th centuries – which prohibited resorting to violence within the *dar-ul-Islam*, and extolled obeisance to authority ('thousand years of tyranny are better than a single minute of anarchy'[5]), even recognized and

[3] See especially his articles in Bernard Lewis, *Le retour de l'Islam*, Paris, Gallimard, 1985, coll. "Nrf"

[4] Cited by Cemil Meriç, *Magaradikl*er, Istanbul, Ötrüken Yayinlari, 1980, p. 1985.

[5] According to Bernard Lewis, this slogan may thus be interpreted: 'An oppressive government must be obeyed [...] because the alternative is worse and because it is only thus that religious prescriptions and legal fundamentals of Islam

legitimized the prince, including the impious, as guarantor of the social order. Henceforth, 'anarchy', as much as 'tyranny' would dominate the history of the two Muslim Empires.

It would be risky to suggest a precise chronological order when recalling the revolutionary passions and expectations that the Middle East had known, since so many cracks in the historical cycle constitute, here as elsewhere, time-space, where diverse political currents, several competitive revolutionary projects branch out before leading on to the bifurcations. After taking this precaution one can still distinguish, from a macro perspective, four successive waves of revolutionary commitment, each registered in a specific political context. The first looks to revolution as the chief purpose of history and at the same time the prerequisite for the regeneration of the two Empires – Ottoman and the Persian. The latter deepens right through the period of Westernization, which covers almost the entire 19th century and extended beyond the First World War. The second that belongs to the inter-War period tries to enter the universal through the radical European movements of the time. The third turned resolutely towards the Left, occupies the Middle Eastern political space after the Second World War to reach its peak at the turn of the 1970s. Finally, the latter decades of the Iranian Revolution of 1979, so full of tragic events, regional wars or massive violence are marked by the Islamist revolutionary axiology and its multiple *avatars*.

1789–1908: REVOLUTIONARY IMAGINATION AND LEGITIMACY

The century-long westernization of the Ottoman, then of the Persian Empire, bears witness to, in the first place, an urgency: to check the 'decline' – a dreaded word no doubt – but no longer

---

are safeguarded'. B. Lewis, *Le langage politique de l'Islam*, Paris, Gallimard, 1988, coll. "Nrf.", p. 153.

a taboo in the political language of the time. It is a time of uncertainties, of multiplication of references and means of rescue, of aborted syntheses as much within an ancient, thousand-year-old local heritage and 'Western thought' as within the diverse currents of ideas coming from Europe. If the necessity for radical reform to reassure the regeneration of the two States is unanimous, it is not enough to overcome the crisis of confidence that the leaders experience within themselves in relation to their models, even in relation to Islam. What to say then of the young, more and more educated in Western ways, even in the West, to whom the Muslim world is simply a desert, without culture, without civilization, without history and, consequently, without a future?

But how to define the West, especially after the Franco-German War of 1870, which shatters the idea of the universal? Then comes the eventful year 1905 when, on the one hand, Socialism emerges as a western alternative enabling the transcending of the West, while, on the other hand, Japan introduces a model of Westernization that does not require a strong self-aversion.[6] If, for someone young, way back in the 1860s, the Western 'order' seemed simple enough to be imported and incorporated in his society, a few decades later, all the frontiers became blurred, and the landmarks, past and present, needed to be redefined, as they refused to reveal their meanings.

The Muslim 'East' gropes along in its imitation of the 'West', itself hesitant in its quest for the future: however, it clings on to some certainties to escape despair. In the first place, the idea that history is teleological, – that is, explaining the past from the origins and consequently leading to the prediction about its future, – ends by making a consensus. Certainly, in the Ottoman Empire (and to a lesser extent in Persia), as in the West, one often adheres only to one of the teleological schools available, from

[6] See Alain Roussillon, *Identité et modernité: les voyageurs égyptiens au Japon (xix–xx siècles)*, Paris, Sindbad, 2005.

social science to religious positivism, from social Darwinism to socialism. But the Khaldounienian[7] cyclical interpretation, which finds in history a permanent strife between a civilization which is sophisticated and a noble barbarism, where the city, conquered by the force of *asabiyya* and a puritan *dawa* let itself be corrupted by the comfort of civilization to become the target of barbarism, is abandoned. History will or will not henceforth be evolutionary and will be with a purpose. In the second place, the idea of revolution, as much a historical necessity as an unchangeable destiny of humanity, gains an intrinsic legitimacy beyond revolutionary circles.[8] Even the most conservative of the European doctrines, like positivism or social science, becomes revolutionary and takes a strong axiological responsibility immediately after crossing the Ottoman frontiers. Finally, in a world which has become obscure, where different scientific and philosophical prophecies compete with one another, a light continues to glitter: 1789, a universal model par excellence in so far as it holds the key to the understanding of the mystery of history. Even the conservative thinkers or the first Salafism which emerges at the turn of the 20th century (and which should not be confused with jihadist Salafism of the period 1990–2000) will challenge these three certainties.

These 'acquired' revolutionaries of the century of Westernization appear differently in the two Muslim empires. The Persian revolution of 1906, which, to a certain extent takes over from Russia of 1905 (which has considerable influence elsewhere), redefines the political vocabulary, from 'justice' to 'consultation', from Islam, from the heritage of the French Revolution and Socialist ideas. The Revolution of 1908 in the Ottoman Empire,

[7] See particularly Gabriel Martinez-Gros, *Ibn Khaldoun et les sept vies de l'Islam*, Arles, Acted Sud, 2006.

[8] On revolution as hope, see Giedre Sabaseviciute, *L'intellectuel et le changement social. Sayyid Qutb: de la réforme sociale à la revolution islamique*, mémoire de Master de l'EHESS, 2008.

which has similarities more with a *pronunciamento* than to a popular revolution, appears as the direct continuation of the French Revolution, even its near-identical answer 'in the East'; moreover, it is highly lauded as such in France. People of 1908, who produce an iconography copied from the French model, also elaborate a charter of agreement in 1789 in order to place themselves on the long temporal scale of the revolution. Has the moment come, wonders one of these men, to constitute the Committee of State Security? They also assign the roles to the point that one of them, the liberal Lütfi Fikri, imagines himself dressed as a Sieyes of the Bosphore before realizing that 'in this country, the Sieyes do not thrive'. Nevertheless identification with the French Revolution is made in a context where one sees a massive shift in the revolutionary imagination, so well that the Turks (and/or the Muslims) are considered as the Third State, repressed and its existence threatened by the Armenian and the Greek[9] 'aristocracy'. Certainly 1908 does not in any way foreshadow the Armenian genocide of 1915; but the legitimization of nationalism by Social Darwinism insidiously prepares the context in which it will become possible.

In Persia, the long revolutionary episode is closed by the counter-revolution of the Palace, but leaves behind a constitutionalist heritage that will later flourish during the political struggles.

In the Ottoman Empire it is the revolution, panic-stricken by the freedom that it itself brought about, which is turned into a counter-revolution to establish *zapt-u-rapt* ('discipline and order'). During this second phase, beginning in 1913, the doctrine of natural rights is 'like a perpetual revolutionary bug, urging people to demand their rights' is strongly condemned, very much like the French Revolution, which set it free from 'Pandora's Box'. The authority will henceforth be obsessed with the wish to have

[9] Hamit Bozarslan, "Allemagne ou France: dualités ottomanes et problème des modèles", *CEMOTI*, nr 12, 1991, pp. 71–98.

citizens who 'shut the eyes, hear the voice that comes to them from the nation and perform their duties'.[10]

BETWEEN THE TWO WARS: FASCINATION FOR THE LEFT AND THE RADICAL RIGHT

The second period begins with the dissolution of the Ottoman Empire and the Russo-British occupation of Persia which pays a rich tribute to the First World War for coming to an end soon after the second global conflict. It envisages the reconfiguration of revolutionary expectations across the Middle East.

In Turkey the victorious Kemalism is considered a full-fledged revolutionary regime, not owing anything to past experiences, either of 1908 or of 1789. Born of the only wish of the man who gave it its name, Mustafa Kemal's widely known ambition was to become in future, with fascist Italy and the Soviet Union, one of the three centres of a non-liberal world. Persia – where Reza Khan succeeds in carrying out a coup d' état, and then proclaims himself the Shah – observes Turkey and over its shoulder, the anti-democratic doctrines of the period between the two Wars. Elsewhere in the Arab world, divided just after the dissolution of the Ottoman Empire, the colonial or representative context determines not only the future of revolutionary passions but also their polarization between a radical Right and an equally radical Left.

The emergence of a Left affiliated to the Communist sphere of influence is slow in the Arab world compared to other parts of the world. For an example, only three Arab delegates are present at the Congress of the People of the East (Baku, September 1920), a pathetic number compared to the huge Turk contingent (235), Persian (192), Armenian (157), even Kurd[11] (8); but the Left in

[10] Z. Gökalp, *Yeni Hayat, Dogru Yol,* Ankara, M.E.B. Yayinlari, 1976, pp. 13–14.

[11] Édith Chabrier, "Les délégués du Premier Congrès des Peuples d'Orient,

Egypt where it is linked with a working class movement opposed to a persistent trade unionism, has a militant tradition born out of the anti-British revolt of 1919, and a strong social visibility. Since 1922, the Egyptian Socialist Party adheres to the 3rd International, only a year after its foundation.[12] Gradually the Communist Left also emerges elsewhere, notably in Syria (1922) and in Iraq (1934), even if it is still far from marking off the political arena and the intellectual debates of these two countries.

The Right and the Left radicals are the new movements since, in spite of some Egyptian antecedents, they do not fall within the framework of the continuity of the rifts between rationalists and liberals or between Occidentalists and Islamists, that had marked the Ottoman space. The frontiers which separate them remain, indeed, fluid, all the more, because national independence constitutes their common objective.

The fact is that the Left is at once characterized by a universalist commitment, which is translated even in the sociological profile of its militants. The non-Muslims who, according to the happy expression used by Talinn Ter Minassian, constitute the 'Hawkers of the Comintern'[13] are present in large numbers in the Left camp. Like the Armenians in Iran and in Turkey, where their number is even more reduced, after the genocide of 1915, the 'minorities' in the Arab world are essentially committed to the core of the Left that offer them double access to the universal, first to the nearest, the dominant Muslim group, then through Moscow, and one often forgets Paris, London or even Berlin, to Europe. The Jewish militants, anti-Zionist in their vast majority, are equally very active within the Left in Iraq or in Egypt. Finally, in this latter

Bakou (1–8 Septembre 1920)", *Cahiers du monde russe et soviétique,* vol. 26, 1985, pp. 21–42.

[12] See Anwar Moghith, "Marxisme égyptien et marxisme occidental: traduction et idéologie", *Égypte, Monde, Arabe,* no. 30-1, 1997, pp. 71–91.

[13] Talinn Ter Minassian, *Colporteurs du Komintern: l'Union soviétique et les minorités au Moyen-Orient,* Paris, Sciences Po, 1997.

country, despite the pre-eminence of the national question, the 'non-nationals' – among who are the Greeks and the Italians – figure among the most active elements of the Communist sphere of influence.[14]

But for all that one should not conclude that the militants of the radical Right or at least of a certain radical nationalism, are all Muslims or that religious adherence necessarily conditions political commitments. The bulk of the militants belonging to the Left is from the Muslim community; conversely, Michel Aflaq, himself a Christian, is radicalized to the point of becoming the real founder of an Arab national socialism, especially after the 'betrayal' of the Popular Front, which does not keep its promises with regard to Syria, then under its control. For him, Islam has importance only with regard to culture and civilization, specifically Arab. Just as the Muslim Brothers, who organize a paramilitary force inspired by the European Right revolutionaries, take recourse to a Koranic legitimacy, other nationalist revolutionary groups, equally organized under the militia, do not have any religious claims.

Yet, in spite of their weak position within the intelligentsia, it is these forces (the Society of the Young Egypt, the paramilitary group of the youth [*al – futuwana*] in Iraq, the boy scouts umeyyades in Syria[15], the different paramilitary organizations in Palestine, like the Association of the young Arab, the National Congress of the Arab youth, the Association of patriotic Arab or even the Association of the Arab boy scouts) who control the 'Arab men in the streets' in the 1930s.

The anti-Semitism, so characteristic of the European radical Right between the two Wars, constitutes, without doubt, one of

[14] See the excellent numbers of the *Cahiers d'histoire. Revue d'histoire critique*, devoted to "Gauches en Égypte, xix–xx centuries" and edited by Didier Monciaud, nos. 105–06, 2008.

[15] Philip Khoury "The Paradoxical Arab Nationalism: Interwar Syria Revisited", in James Jankowski and Israel Gershomi, *Rethinking Nationalism in the Arab Middle East*, New York, Columbia University Press, 1997, p. 277.

the reasons of the appeal of the radical Right in the Arab world but marginally and only in the opinion of people like Rashid Ali al-Gaylani, an Iraqi putschist of 1941 or Haj Amin al-Husseini, the great Mufti, well-known in Jerusalem.[16] As Reinhard Schulze sums it up:

> The ideals of the Muslim Right closely correspond to those of Italian fascism under Mussolini, with its corporatist system of social representation and idealization of history. National Socialism, which is inseparable from racism and anti-Semitism [...] was, since the beginning, a marginal phenomenon in the Muslim world.[17]

The radical Right has tended to look elsewhere than towards anti-Semitism in order to move forward in the search for unity of the Arab world. The latter was first harmed by the break-up of the country by the French and the British after the First World War. Later, the very viability given to Arab 'kingdoms' comes at the expense of the long cherished dream of national unity. The international, cosmopolitan nature of the Left in the inter-War period, contrasts with the response of exclusive nationalist stand of the Right who in mobilizing forces, shows a discursive one-upmanship.[18]

According to Furet's[19] definition of ' the particular opposed to the universal' and the 'people against class', the nationalist Right cannot lean on international solidarity advocated by the Komintern. It is nevertheless a fact that like the Left, it can take advantage of its scientific credibility regarded as irrefutable by a number of learned scholars on the subject across Europe. The Left

[16] Gerhard Höpp, *Mufti Papiren, Briefe, Memoranden, Reden und Anrufe Amin al-Husseinis aus dem Exil*, Berlin, Schiller Verlag, 2002.

[17] Reinhard Schulze, *A Modern History of the Islamic World*, New York, New York University Press, 2002, p. 107.

[18] See the Symposium entitled, 'L'experience sovietique et le problème national dans le monde, 1920–1939, Langues-O, 1978, 2 vols.

[19] François Furet, *Penser le xx siècle*, Paris, Robert Laffont, 2007, p. 534.

subscribes to a 'philosophy of history' that judges human life by the yardstick of Social Darwinism – in other words a war among nations resembles a war between biological species.

The reasons for Arab decline, today had its origins well before European occupation and the foreign domination in the present age can be explained in a similar fashion.

The Nationalist right shows the route to consolidating itself by forming a strong authoritarian structure of national unity. It identifies the external, European enemy, as well as its domestic 'lackeys' but avoids bloody class struggles since the ostensible aim is national unity.

The radical Right considers it has at its disposal a further reason for superiority in relation to the Left. Besides its scientific assets, it wishes to add the quality of 'mysticism' in which 'the nation transforms into a natural aristocracy consisting of certain endowed individuals-genius and superman'.[20] It is equally fascinated by war as the natural arena for self and nation.

To take an example, in 1933, Sami Shawkat who replaced the romantic Arab nationalist Sati' al-Husri in the post of the director of education, explains that a 'nation which does not openly proclaim death by the sword and the fire will perish under the hooves of horses and the boots of foreign armies [...] it is our duty to perfect the proclamation of death, of the army and the sacred military.'[21] The response to Shawkat comes from Michel Aflaq several decades later, while in practice, almost no one then adheres overtly to a nationalism of the Right:

> In our time the Arab revolution merges with war because the latter offers the most important, the fullest and the safest ground

[20] Hannah Arendt, *Les origins du totalitarianism, Imperialisme,* Paris, Le Seuil, 1984, p. 104.

[21] Peter Sluglett, "Le Parti Ba'ath: Panarabisme, national-socialisme et dictature", in Chris Kutschera, *Le Livre noir de Saddam Hussein*, Paris, Oh! Éditions, 2005, p. 91.

> for the blossoming of our talents, our abilities and our heroism. Pushed to its extreme consequences the civilization we are trying to establish can only survive by fighting, that is to say, by armed battle of the people.[22]

This eulogy to physical strength, of the superman and of immortality conquered by death, given and received, which had so much characterized the mood between the two Wars, could not remain indifferent to a Middle East, obsessed with the national question and already so fully integrated with Europe.

1965–1989: RADICALISMS OF THE LEFT

With the fall of fascist Italy, then of the Nazi Germany, the Middle East enters a new period where the Left appears as the ascending political force so much as to appeal to a large number of nationalist militants, like Michael Aflaq and the Ba'ath party which he (re)builds in 1947. Outside Libya, where it is supported by the army (Katïb, founded in 1936), practically none of the parties claims anymore to adhere to the radical Right. The reasons for this success are related at the same time to the Soviet Union and to the transformations in the Arab world itself. François Furet explains in *The Past of an Illusion* that the tremendous sacrifice made by the Soviet people during the Second World War, then the end of the Nazi nightmare in Europe, made one forget the horrors of the Stalinist terror and had considerably enhanced the prestige of the USSR. The land of the proletariat is thus transformed into an eulogy of anti-fascism and peace. During the course of the immediate post-War years, the repercussions of this international fame are equally visible in a Middle East where the Soviet Union plays an increasingly active role. After having sustained the creation of the state of Israel, and thus provoking

[22] Michel Aflaq, *Choix des texts de la pensée du fondateur du parti Ba'ath. Unité-Liberté-Socialisme*, Madrid, s.n., 1977, p. 88.

wrath of the Arab nationalists and weakening the communist parties in the region, the USSR sides with the Arab world against 'Imperialism and Zionism'. While continuing with the thesis already put forward by the Comintern, the Kremlin elaborates a new foreign policy favouring national or bourgeois revolutions – steps necessary before the 'Great Eve'*, supposed to lead to the socialist revolution. This opening up reinforces its appeal to multiple radicalisms, both social and national.

It must be said that that more than twenty years after the end of the First World War, which had completely reconfigured these countries, the political agenda of the Middle East is still dominated by the national question. The independence won forcibly in Paris and London is only a formal one and to aggravate the situation, a force in many respects more aggressive than the former European powers, namely the United States, is henceforth active in the region. Likewise, and I will come back to it, the creation of the state of Israel is perceived by Arab public opinion as a veritable amputation carried out by the 'imperialist West.'

In this context Franz Fanon's superb analysis, as precise as it is naive, of African expectations, turns out to be equally pertinent to the Middle East:

> The Americans should know that if they wish to fight against communism, they must, in certain sectors, adopt communist attitudes. For the colonial people, enslaved by the Western nations, the communist countries are the only ones who have always stood by them. The colonial countries are not interested to know if this attitude is dictated by the relevance of the communist strategy; all that they remember is that this general tendency is in their own interest. The colonial people are not really communists but they are implacably anti-colonial.[23]

[23] Franz Fanon, *Pour la révolution africaine. Écrits politiques*, Paris, La Découverte, 2006, p. 111.

* Communist terminology to explain the eve of the uprising of the working classes in the Revolution. Editor.

Indeed, Fanon states that 'communism' need not depend on warning signs to disseminate ideas; shortly the emergence of the Third World, promising everyone a place under the sun, will embrace the faith. However, his analysis does not do justice to all the complexities of the African situations, and by analogy, to those of the dominated parts of the world. Indeed, if the national question occupies such a centrality in the anti-establishment subjectivities, it is because it is also supposed to hold the key to the rest. Generations of Left do not abandon the quest for emancipation promised by the 'Enlighteners'*, nor the longing for justice, but they think that their aspirations are hindered by those very people who they extol. 'Imperialism' and its 'lackeys', never short of coercive measures to impose their order, allow inequalities of classes, religious archaism, obscurantism, even 'feudalism' to endure. Strictly speaking, communism appears at the time to be the only means to realize these Western promises against the West.

Already, in the years between 1920 and 1930, the aristocratic and bureaucratic elites, products of the Ottoman Empire, were no longer in tune with their society. This rupture is aggravated after the Second World War. While the Middle East opens up to the world, the new intelligentsia no longer shares the same references with the ageing power structure. Westernization, in their opinion, had failed to bring about either independence or economic and social development.

Some members of this intelligentsia are plebian by birth, pure products of an education system conceived by the West or the local elites; but they are acutely aware of the existence of the underprivileged classes and the extent of their misery. Others are children of well-known urban residents, known for their conservatism but they detest their parents' generation as much as the system with which they associate them. Of course, the world

* Les Lumières refers to the leading lights of the Enlightenment of the 18th century. Editor.

in which this intelligentsia develops is neither civil nor bourgeois in the sense in which François Furet uses it, while speaking about European communism.

The Arab city is not more vulnerable or even threatened because the young refuse to join the ruling classes. The young generation knows that the only way to achieve their night of 4 August is to abandon their own class and thus unite the nation. The fund of knowledge they have gained about militancy and sacrifice in the barricades is the prerequisite for their participation in the new nation and society. The Left offers a variety of national and international routes to this, as well as 'a new symbolic cadre that can formulate and think of political problems and react accordingly'.[24]

Indeed, the Left brings with it categories of diverse analyses giving meaning to the conflicts that it stimulates in return. It denounces the present age, finds it guilty of the decline of human beings, resulting in oppression, corruption and of national servitude; but it also falls prey to waning forces such as 'imperialism' and its 'lackeys' who block the future nation where they do not belong. It links two kinds of conflicts; the first is national and anti-imperialist, that carries the promise of emancipation of the oppressed people, and the second social, since its ultimate aim is the freedom of the human condition. The coexistence of these two categories allows its followers to belong at the same time to the people and to the oppressed classes. Finally, the Left assures at the same time continuity with Westernization as well as its rupture. It preserves the idea of progress and offers instruments of criticism of the existing order in all its constituent elements, including tradition and religion where it does not take a soft line.[25]

As in the latter instance it emanates from the West, it legitimizes the confrontation with it as a condition of the construction of the

[24] Clifford Geertz, "Ideology as a Cultural System", in David Apter (ed.) *Ideology and Discontent,* New York, The Free Press, 1964, p. 65.

[25] See particularly the articles of Gustav E. von Grünebaum collected in his work, *L'identité culturelle de l'Islam*, Paris, Gallimard, 1969.

universal. Pure and simple Westernization, that of grandparents and parents, needed denial of the self and of its history in order to become a part of history. Thus, if the Left continues to deny the national past, responsible for the decline, it also provides a criticism of Western history that is marked, right from start to finish, by oppression and domination, in the dialectic of the master and the slave. With the alliance that it promises between the people oppressed by the West and the oppressed classes of the West, it helps to come out of this double past, its own and that of its enemy, and it helps to liberate itself from the alienation which is consubstantial to it, to attain universal emancipation.

How does one place class struggles in this context? The answer to this question is more complex than it appears at first sight. The predominance of the national question does not systematically invalidate class-based contestation. In Turkey, Iraq and Egypt, countries where a tradition of trade unionism exists, there is a strong mobilization of the working class, while the countryside witnesses a real struggle for emancipation by the peasantry. Elsewhere, this is only a marginal case. Certainly, the leftist and the communist commitment find its ultimate reference in the proletariat and the promise of a bright future, after the formation of a class-less society. Dedicating itself to its own dissolution to attain the end of its struggle, the proletariat sets the tone of the protest without necessarily committing itself to the struggle. And for a good reason: often it is nonexistent or numerically too weak to influence the problems of the world. Since then, the communist sphere of influence can only count on the educated classes, whether they are of plebian origin but already a part of the 'petty bourgeoisie' or emanating from the urban upper classes or from the bureaucracy.

This intelligentsia, whose vocation is to 'carry history on its back'[26] and to open the way to emancipation, is seen as the avant-garde of the proletariat to which it does not belong. The

[26] The expression is of Sayyid Uways, *L'histoire que je porte sur le dos ...*, Marseille, Parenthèses, 2006.

sociological as well as the philosophical discrepancy, between the status and the historic mission that it sets for itself, becomes bearable thanks to the doctrinaire subtleties of Leninism which distinguishes the 'real' proletariat from the Party incarnating its 'conscience' and, therefore, being empowered to act in its name.

In the end one can very well make a distinction between class struggle and the social question. If the communist parties brandish the slogan of class struggle, the non-communist Left appears to be timid on this subject which divides the nation. Nevertheless, it remains sensitive to the social question and knows the necessity of practical measures to alleviate the sufferings of millions of destitutes. In the three countries (Egypt, Syria and Iraq) to which we shall come back, young officers of the Left will deploy a policy of allocation of resources (free education, healthcare, freezing of rate of interest, agrarian reforms ...) since their coming to power. Though it is aware of the 'egalitarian urgency', the non-communist Left, however, thinks that national injustice, imposed on the entire nation by imperialism and colonialism, is the source of social injustice. If the problems, social, economic, political and national, are various and have become more acute with the passage of time, they all emanate from a single cause, of a Gordian Knot whose threads can only be disentangled by the sword of revolution.

ARAB REVOLUTIONARY REGIMES

From the time the State of Israel was founded in 1948, the Arab Middle East enters a period of open protest that can be described as a revolutionary crisis, even if it ends, – I shall come back to it, – not by revolutions but by urban revolts, one after another, and coups d'état. Indeed, the *Naqba*, a real experience, new amputation of the Arab world and the intermediary step of a long-term programme of colonization, radicalizes public opinion more than the Franco-British division of the Arab world between 1919 and 1920.

The revolutionary crisis, of which the revolts, called *intifada* or *watbah* are the most visible manifestations, is, above all, this moment when the fear of repression disappears to make room for anger and axiological perseverance. The scenes of insurrection of the years 1940 and 1950 are part of the continuity of the revolts, suppressed forcibly, of the decade between 1920 and 1930. But an urban revolt, often the consequence of spontaneity and indecisiveness, sustained from day to day by the dynamics that it triggers off, is quite different from the classic armed, clandestine revolts with long-term roots.

Indeed, it mobilizes unarmed civilians against a heavily armed coercive order. The crushing of a revolt marks its temporary end; anything can spark yet another revolt in the same period. Whatever be the cause, even for a short while, this crushing names a certain victor, the power and the vanquished. The repression of a revolt creates a situation of chronic instability where the authorities must negotiate its day to day legitimacy, since as it is incapable of restoring fear as the ultimate 'tool of governance', thereby reclaiming victory, howsoever temporary, of a coercive system.

Another major trait distinguishes the revolts between 1920 and 1930 from the riots of 1940 to 1950: apart from the Egyptian revolt of 1919, which had mobilized the cities and its outskirts and the cities equally well, the revolts of the past decades were marked by the pre-eminence of the elites who can be defined as traditionalists; some of whom eventually accepted the game and terms of co-optation played by the people in power.

Often localized, these revolts did not necessarily affect the capitals. The riots of the years 1940 and 1950, on the other hand, were led by the urban youth, particularly the students, the intelligentsia, – both civil and military – and took place right in the capital.

The mobilization of the young and the intelligentsia translates the incapacity of the political order to reproduce itself by the transmission of its values to the next generations. The participation of the military signifies that the organs constituted by those in power and responsible for their protection, organs which have so often and so effectively exercised coercion against society, had ceased to obey the orders of the Prince. More than the praetorian force of the city, henceforth the military aims at becoming the first consuls. While the instability and lack of law and order originates in authority itself, the brutality of the repression can only reduce the power into an alienated force, which does not engage with society.

The crisis of legitimacy and obedience similarly produces another consequence: the powers become quite simply incapable of clarifying the categories and differing roles of one another, of distinguishing a friend from a foe, of identifying the lawful and the unlawful. In certain cases they strive hard to overcome this crisis by identifying the Jews of the Arab world as their enemies, thus fuelling the anti-Semitism campaigns that they, however, will not be able to utilize to their advantage. As for their anger with regard to Israel, it turns out to lack conviction, since none among them is able to protect Palestine or ensure its survival without Western support. Public opinion however continues to find the West guilty of being the root cause of the original division of territory in 1948.

Henceforth, the ability to define the enemy is passed on to the man in the street which finds it to be two-fold: imperialism and its internal 'lackeys', reactionary forces, capitalist or feudal. Indeed, in the eyes of the Opposition, imperialism, the external enemy, cannot act without the complicity of the internal enemy which thus becomes a traitor to its own family.

Two Prime Ministers, in Syria and in Egypt, and a King, in Jordan, will pay with their lives for this 'betrayal' in the years following the creation of the state of Israel; another King and another Prime Minister, this time Iraqi, will get a reprieve of ten years before being executed in 1958.

In spite of mobilization of the communist parties, the spearhead of the protest, especially in Iraq and in Egypt and other forces of

Muslim brotherhood, the revolutionary crisis will push a single actor to the front of the stage: the army[27].

There is no doubt that their seizure of power in Egypt (1952), in Syria (in 1949, then in 1963), in Iraq (1958), and in a very different context in Libya (1969), resembles military coups d' état rather than popular revolutions. Yet these political putsches are quite different from those one witnesses in the years between 1950 and 1960 in Latin America. Indeed, the intensity of the revolutionary crisis has radicalized the military which intervenes to take over civil protest movements rather than perpetuating an oligarchic power; incapable of seizing power themselves, the civil actors agree to proceed by delegating and legitimizing the military, greeted as the saviour, to entrust it with the explicit mission of solving the 'national question'.

This renunciation of the common man, of action and power just after the military coup explains why military regimes initially enjoyed a certain popularity. It is true that there is no mystery or anything secretive about the military's authoritarian ambitions nor of their demand for consensus and obedience; but in a context where the 'bourgeois democracy' is accused of being a trap set by the West to weaken the Arab world, and this has lost all its credibility[28], their programme can only lead to adherence.

Is authoritarianism not the only system providing the nation with the strength it so desperately needs? Does it not help to rally together around the national resources suspending the arbitrary conflicts and class struggles thanks to a policy of redistribution, always insufficient but still bold? Does consensus not mobilize the nation in its fight against 'imperialism, Zionism and their internal collaborators', responsible for the defeat and dishonour of the

[27] For a global reading of the "modernist" and "economist" in these revolutions see Enver M. Koury, *The Patterns of Mass Movements in Arab Revolutionary Progressive States*, La Haye, Mouton, 1970.

[28] See Matthieu Rey, *Le moment électorale de 1954 en Syrie et en Irak, étude sur le pluralism politique au Moyen-Orient*, mémoire de master de l'EHESS, 2009.

nation? Paradoxically, it is by the destruction of all democratic perspectives demanding pluralities and internal cleavages that the power in the Arab world will gain temporarily a true legitimacy.

But at what price? The appraisal of the 'revolutionary regimes' or 'Arab socialism' will turn out to be disastrous in the long run especially there where they had themselves raised the standards high: they will not be able to keep their promises of uniting the nation to make it strong enough to enjoy freedom: sunk into oblivion (is) the development of the Arab world without even talking of 'the liberation of Palestine'! As the Tunisian President Habib Bourguiba says with his characteristic irony, 'never have the Arabs killed one another as ferociously since Nasser took upon himself the sacred mission of uniting[29] them.' Each regime, worn down by internal strife, quickly takes root in the logic of principality, inherited from colonialism to the detriment of Pan-Arab unity promised to their societies.

In two decades the military regimes will be transformed either into bureaucratic dictatorship (Egypt) or into a coalition of military and intelligence service (Syria), even into totalitarianism (Iraq), placing the communist parties to face the Cornelian dilemma of cooperating with them at the risk of ceasing to exist as autonomous forces or of passing again to the Opposition, even if it means being called traitors of the nation and getting themselves eliminated. They will make the first choice while steering clear of the firebrands, the 'revolutionary princes.' In Egypt, for example, one witnesses the 'Nasserization' of Marxism during the 'Marxization' of Nasserism[30]; in spite of this compromise the communists will share the hardships of detention camps with

[29] Cited by François Massouilié, *Les Conflits du Proche-Orient. XX siècle*, Paris, Casterman-Giunti, 1994, p. 86.

[30] Sherif Younis, 'Marxisme et patriotisme dans les régimes militaires de libération nationale: les officiers libres et les "communists égyptiens" ', *Cahiers d'histoire. Revue d'histoire critique*, issues dedicated to the "Gauches en Égypte xix–xx siécles", edited by Didier Monciaud, nos. 105–06, 2008, pp. 157–59.

the Muslim Brothers. Many of them will be sentenced to years of imprisonment and torture in Syria[31] and the Communist Party of Iraq, the most powerful in the Arab world, will be purely and simply liquidated by Saddam Hussein in 1979[32]. The USSR, which provides unwavering support to the 'Arab revolutionary regimes' and assures them security and an economic subsidy, will remain quiet about it.

THE PLURALITY OF THE LEFT

The emergence of these military regimes which dilutes the 'socialism' within Arab nationalism is not the only manifestation of the swing of the Middle East to the Left. Elsewhere in the region, a large number of youth and the intelligentsia also find there the clue to their oppressed condition and the road map of liberation. The appeal of communism will become increasingly strong all through the 1950s, without being affected by the incidents as great as the revelations of Khruschev at the 20th Congress of the Communist Party of the USSR (1956) or the crushing of the Hungarian revolt (the same year). The star that becomes tarnished at home and partially also in Europe continues to shine in the Middle East, which is so near and yet so distant.

The paradox, in this shift to the Left, is that the USSR has, in fact, nothing much to do there. Since the disappearance of the Comintern and, especially after the death of Stalin, Moscow does not act any more as the 'direct political agitator' in the region, and the support provided to the communist movements is minimal. We have witnessed wherever the military Left grabs power, the USSR agrees to abandon the communist parties to their lot. In Turkey and in Iran, two countries forming with Israel the strategic

[31] See, for example, Yassin al-Haj Saleh, "L'univers des anciens prisoniers politiques en Syrie", *REMMM*, no. 115–116, 2007, pp. 249–65.

[32] See Chris Kutschera, *Le Livre noir de Saddam Hussein*, Paris, Oh! Éditions, 2005.

American axis in the region, practice a policy of accommodation and economic cooperation; its contribution to the struggle of the communist parties of these countries being to welcome its leaders in one of the satellite countries of Eastern Europe.

In reality, the success of the communist Left comes from the fact that it set into action the multiple and autonomous dynamics of opposition protest, which was the message from its transmitting source.

In the course of time, the languages of commitment to the Left also became plural so as to no longer depend exclusively on the 'voice of Moscow.' Since the beginning of the 1960s, and especially after the Cultural Revolution in China, the ideas of the Left are propagated by the impact of Maoism, more and more openly anti-Soviet. In the course of this decade, the 'Guevarist' model or the theories of the *foco* will always play a role more important than all the Soviet propaganda in the passage to radicalism in the Middle East. After the death of Mao, the 'Enverism'*, proclaimed by Albania, will similarly experience short-lived glory in more than one country of the Middle East. There again, one must not look for the hand of Beijing or of Tirana which goes as far as to ignore the very existence of their distant disciples, or refuse to maintain any relation with them in order not to compromise their relations with their neighbours.

However that may be, in symbolic terms the USSR is the greatest loser of this 'pluralization' of the Left, even if, in reality, it is least concerned about it. The growing disillusionment of the Middle East with the USSR has nothing to do with the internal history of communism. The 'superpower' of the East disappoints by its cynicism as much as the United States; whether it conducts *realpolitik* in relation to the repressive United States, thus failing *ad minima* to perform its duty of international solidarity, or

* This term is derived from the name of the Albanian President, Enver Xoxa. Editor.

whether it supports the Arab revolutionary regimes at the risk of being taken for an imperialist power (even 'social-imperialist', to use the Maoist term), exploiting the resources of these countries. Heavily implicated in regional politics and embodied in a gerontocracy, it has lost its aura to appeal and responds to the 'ideological lacunae'[33] in the Middle East; instead, distant China with its mobilized masses and the Little Red Book fills this gap.

Likewise over bureaucratization of the USSR is reproduced within the regional communist parties which become like an inert apparatus and an easy prey considering the coercion of the pro-Soviet revolutionary Arab states. In contrast, China is supposed to offer, through the Cultural Revolution, a 'non-bureaucratic' model of a truly 'participatory' communism. This passage to an 'alternative communism' provokes in the first place, a cleavage within the intelligentsia, followed by a generational rift within the entire Left movement. The sociological profile of the young who join the opposition in the 1970s, will particularly be very different from that of the older generation; for these newcomers who have been born in radical times, Maoism will seem exotic as well as serve as a discourse on legitimization. It will lead them into plebeian-rooted politics and it will offer them the modes of rupture with previous generations.

CONTESTED TERRITORIES

Two minority spaces, supra-territorial and cross-border, the Palestinian and the Kurd respectively, are particularly sensitive to the appeal of the Left and especially of the plurality of its languages. The first, which popularizes the notion of *thawra,* is dominated by 'progressive' actors since the end of the 1950s; the second, which takes recourse to the term *chorech,* becomes the

[33] Maxime Rodinson, *Marxisme et le monde musulman*, Paris, Le Seuil, 1972, p. 311

horizon of expectations for the Kurdish protest from the 1960s. The exile of 1948, then that of 1967, dispersed the Palestinians towards the Middle East where they formed themselves into political groups and as an intermediary of transmission and diffusion and modes of anti-establishment action. The division of their territories into three zones of the Middle East – Arab, Iranian and Turk – makes the Kurds a 'nomadic group' at the regional level. Despite the differences in their conditions, the two spaces have a quasi-spontaneous penchant for a universal Left, advocating internationalism, namely, emancipation, mobility and multiple adherences. In both the cases, that which can be called 'Marxist universalism' (XXS, 540), helps the national struggles to start explaining their situation of subordination, promising the people emancipation by giving them the right to decide for themselves, and open at the same time the road to a new universal Left through the alliance one was so hoping for, with the oppressed classes of the oppressor states. Thus, while challenging the legitimacy of the state of Israel, the Palestine Liberation Organization (PLO) of Yasser Arafat clearly distances itself from anti-Semitism and envisages its future as tri-confessional, one might as well say, confessional. The opposition of the Kurds, often showing solidarity with the 'Arab revolution', is neither anti-Arab nor anti-Persian nor anti-Turk any more.

Though cherishing zealously the idea of a Palestine or of a Kurdistan, the militants, born of these groups, replace the Christians and the Jews whose numbers diminish drastically in the Middle East as 'hawkers' of the ideas of the Left. Someone of the type of Leyla Khaled (and that of, quite less known, Leyla Quassem, a Kurd student executed in 1974 at the age of 22) shows that entry into this universal is at the cost not only of battles, past and present, of sacrifices made for national emancipation, but also for the justice and freedom of the human genre as a whole. The Palestinian resistance which arouses such great sympathy across the world appeals, sometimes for the better and often for the worse, to the militants of the radical Left for whom Arafat is the Arab counterpart of 'Che'. More religious in its ambitions, also more classical in the forms that it assumes, the Kurdish protest in Iraq is perceived as one of the anti-colonial guerilla movements, the most important in the 1960s. As internal intermediaries between these two minority spaces, a number of Kurds participate in the Palestinian struggle, which has become the melting pot of the armed protests at the regional level, particularly in Jordan and in Libya.

Apart from these territories outside state control, mention should be made of the spaces, somewhat peripheral, of the Arab world, beginning with Sudan where the 'free officers' come to power following the Egyptian model (1956) to herald the era of an Arab and African 'socialism'. The dictatorship of Jaafar Nimeiri, their leader, in September 1971, leads to a massive repression of the communists, formerly his principal allies, thus wiping out one of the most powerful communist parties of the Arab and African world. Yemen, divided since 1893, is wrought by a social radicalism, aimed at 'not only the colonial power but also the political elites and social natives'.

> The role of the popular movements organized by the radical political parties there may have been more important than (it is) elsewhere, partly because of the more rigid social structures [...], and partly because of the absence of intermediary institutions like the modernized armed forces which played such a big role in other Arab states.[34]

In Dhofar, the breakaway guerrilla group of the Marxist national democratic front for the liberation of Oman and the

[34] Fred Halliday, "The Formation of Yemeni Nationalism: Initial Reflections", in James Jankowski and Israel Gershomi, *Rethinking Nationalism in the Arab Middle East*, New York, Columbia University Press, 1997, p. 34. See also the authorised memoir of Franck Mermier, *Une anthropolgie du fait urbain dans l'orient arabe*, preparé sous le tutorat de Dionigi Albera, université de Marseille-Aix-en-Provence, 2010.

Persian Gulf, launched in 1963, continues for a decade and comes to an end with the surrender of the insurgents in 1976.[35]

Further West, in Maghreb, the Left becomes the hegemonic syntax within the intelligentsia and produces its *tribuniciens* which sometimes enjoy a certain immunity, and are sometimes victims of a fierce repression. In Algeria, the National Liberation Front (FLN), which is introduced as the only keeper of revolutionary legitimacy, monopolizes the entire political space and leaves little scope for activities to an autonomous radical Left. In Tunisia, 'bourgeuibism' is conceived as a progressive revolution by those in power, who are in fear of Pan-Arab nationalism as well as of the radical Left. If it does not deploy a heavily repressive policy, it does not hesitate either to take recourse to intimidating measures against Left intellectuals, some of whom are tortured or imprisoned. In Morocco, on the other hand, the group of Muhammad Bennouna, comprising immigrants, of 'proletariats', and of traders and businessmen, is radicalized along with the sanctification of monarchy. The battle that continued from 1963 to 1973 will come to an end by the physical elimination of its leaders[36], imprisonment of long duration and internal[37] or external exile of the surviving members.

Finally, a few words on the non-Arab Muslim world: the young and a large section of the intelligentsia are won over by the Left in Iran, where a strong tradition of revolutionary protest has existed since 1910. The repression of 1953, which accompanied the coup d' état against Mossadegh, organized by the CIA, then

[35] For reference on this war, see Fred Halliday, *Arabia without Sultans*, London, Penguin, 1974.

[36] Mehdi Benounna, *Héros sans gloire. Échec d'une revolution 1963–1973*, Casablanca, Tarek Éditions, 2002.

[37] Mounia Bennani-Chraibi, "Parcours, cercles et médiations à Casablanca. Tous les chemins mènent à l'action associative de quartier", in Mounia Bennani-Chraibi et Olivier Fillieule (eds.), *Résistances et protestations dans les sociétés musulmanes*, Paris, Sciences Po, 2003, pp. 293–352.

the massacres of 1963, had not only paralyzed the Tudeh, the pro-Soviet Communist party (like the rest of the liberal and Islamist opposition), but it had also convinced the youth of the impossibility of achieving a social transformation by peaceful means. As a Leftist journal of 1974 remembers: 'From then on the militants abandoned ideology and asked themselves the question *what is to be done?* The answer was clear; fight the army'.[38] It will be started by the young, hardly 25 years old, and it will be carried on till the revolution of 1979, at the cost of a heavy repression, leaving thousands of people dead. In Turkey, where the tradition of commitment to the Left had partially died out with the sharp decline in the number of minority Christians and Jews, one witnesses in the 1960s a strange honeymoon between Kemalism and the Left; at first peaceful, the latter, in order to turn in favour of the coups d' état of 1971 and 1980, becomes radicalized after the repression which begins in 1968. There, again, the coercive policy of Ankara and the confrontations (including with the radical Right) will leave thousands of victims.

Finally, further in the Muslim world, other regions turn radical: Pakistan, as shown in the remarkable film *Khamosh Pani* (2003) by Sabiha Sumar, experiences an incredible mobilization of the young towards the Left (at times sustained by a section of the political class); in Afghanistan, where before going into a gory internal war, which appears as a prelude to the Soviet occupation of 1979, two branches of the communist party, *Khalq* (People) and *Parcham* (Flag), co-exist and are in negotiation with a section of the army.

PROFILES OF MILITANCY

Despite their specificities, according to the areas taken into consideration, the Left militants during these long decades share

[38] *Mojahed* cited by Yann Richard, *L'Iran. Naissance d'une république islamique*, Paris, La Martinière, 2006, p. 288.

a number of traits with their homologues across the world. The understanding of this continuum calls for comparative studies, badly needed at the moment. As hypothesis, one can, however, specify that the spread of communism, especially in the years 1960 and 1970, stems as much from a symbolic and an iconographic whole, widely standardized, as from a simplified vulgate, by extension any doctrine, epitomizing the creed in a few key ideas like the war of the classes, fight against obscurantism, moral proletarian verses, moral bourgeoisie, etc.

The battle fought and the sacrifices made across the planet are reflected in the same mirrors, because the universal is built and measured by the participation of all and sundry with a common goal. The available support, visual as well as emotional, to the 'comrades', both from within and without, turns out to be the foundation of a true international language and creates a republic of commitment, whose members are known to one another, even if they are not able to speak to one another directly. Even this obstacle is partially removed thanks to a frenetic activity of translation, at times professional, more often amateurish and spontaneous, which even the most repressive measures are not able to curb. One must, in fact, remember that the Left is also the crucible where the know-how and the ways to become an intellectual – by arguing and debating the choice of favorite subjects related to social issues – are learnt. With variations explicable by each local history, the 'Little library of the perfect communist' of the Middle East in the 1960s or in the 1970s would, without doubt, resemble the one found in Latin America. It would provide the explanation, the response and the future scenario on a vast number of subjects, ranging from the condition of women to the question of housing.[39]

[39] Apart from the writings which focus on agrarian economy, there are a few pieces written by Marxist intellectuals of the time, marked by their high standard. Let us, however, keep in mind that several intellectuals were inspired by Marxism and at the same time they were critical of it, remembered among

Here, as elsewhere in the world, commitment gives rise to circles of social groups, formed by sacrifice, the history of which is marked by the martyrdom of a number of figures, particularly in Iraq, Turkey, Iran or even Morocco. Other divisive elements include suspicions, betrayals, 'change of camps' and, of course, the dramatic internal fragmentation provoking internal splits of the Left into dozens of rival organizations. It is true that within each organization there is a rule of disciplinary order which often has no reason to envy the powers and traditions of the order, denounced as obscurantist, that it is fighting against; but commitment to the Left is no less an act of emancipation, especially for women and the young. The greatness of the cause for which they agree to fight, provides women the arms of resistance, morally superior, against male domination. Indeed, in the feminist battle, so to say, this 'marriage with the revolution' demands personal sacrifice and renunciation of one's stand on matters of sex.

The emancipation of the female sex is, indeed, conditioned by that of the human genre and, consequently delayed till the realization of the latter.

Equally, youth finds in this fight a way of struggling against parental discipline. This 'youthful' definition of the world leads it to consider itself a protagonist to bring about the regeneration of the former crepuscular world. It offers its own body as a sacrificial site of collective suffering, to get rid of a society based on authority, outmoded wisdom and the window dressing of the master-slave relationship in social relations. Youth offers up the body of the leader (like Arafat) as the model for the new Man.

---

whom are Idris Küçükömer (Turkey), Ali al-Wardi (Iraq), Abdallah Laroui (Morocco), Dariush Shayegan (Iran), or even the Palestinian Edward Said, whose writings are original and extensive. Likewise,as seen from the correspondence of Maxime Rodinson, certain Marxists in the Middle East kept alive a debate of quality with their European counterparts. See M. Rodinson, *Marxisme et le monde musulman*, Paris, Le Seuil, 1972.

THE IRANIAN REVOLUTION OR THE CONTRACTION OF THE UNIVERSAL

Rare are the years that one can unhesitatingly point at as the dates of a radical rupture; 1979 is one of them, as it changes the order in the history of the revolutionary passions in the Middle East. While the Syrian and the Iraqi Ba'ath, who had sometimes cherished the hope of Arab resistance in the Middle East, expose themselves more and more as being coercive and bureaucratic regimes, primarily concerned with ensuring their tenure, the peace agreements between Israel and Egypt sound the death knell for the experience of 'Arab socialism' launched by the army.

After occupying Afghanistan at the end of the year, the USSR places itself among the imperialist powers which threaten the Muslim world in the same way as the United States or the former colonizers did. At the same time, the gradual exit of China from Maoist precepts reduces its appeal to zero, particularly as the magnet for a new world left movement.

On the other hand, an Islamist insurrection at Mecca that the Saudi authorities are able to crush thanks to the intervention of the French GIGN, and particularly the Iranian Revolution, demonstrate the capability of Islamism to transform itself into a revolutionary intermediary in the region.

Independent of one another, these four incidents change the destiny of the Middle East so much that they are interpreted in terms of radicalized subjectivity of the region and of an 'axiological urgency', not lacking in density. The incidents of this incredible year, which establish betrayal and history as the two essential components of a philosophy of hitherto unpublished history, cannot most certainly arouse revolutionary passions. The double 'betrayal' of Egypt and of the USSR, that is to say, of the Arab nationalist Left and by capillarity of the Arab internationalist Left, validate *a posteriori* the criticisms of Sayeed Qotb, the Islamist thinker, executed by the Nasserist regime in 1966. The Iranian

Revolution proves that the enemies – in this instance the most powerful among them being the United States, are not invincible – and confirms once again the sharpness of this thinker who had exposed the illusion of the *taghuti* (polytheist) world.

The Palestinian and the Kurdish spaces continue to be anchored in the Left for yet another long period but the 'charm of October', to borrow Furet's favourite expression, is dramatically shattered elsewhere in the region. The Left was still so powerful in the decade of 1970 that it practically monopolized the intellectual debate, and the horizon of hope is, within the space of a year, reduced to an anachronistic fact.

Quite a few of its militants will go into exile clinging to nostalgia to take up the pen again after years in order to put their societies on their guard against authoritarianism of the powerful *and* against Islamism[40]; others will convert themselves to the new ideology, by opportunism, or more often by the concern for giving a new meaning to the years of strife and sacrifice. How can they, indeed, remain outside the revolutionary fervour which certainly makes their past ideological convictions look obsolete, but on the other hand reward so magnificently their moral commitment?

Here it is not necessary to put emphasis on the revolutionary crisis in Iran, during which for two years the Left organizations played a decisive role before being ousted with a rare violence by the supporters of Khomeini. Outside factual history, which is well-known, this revolution presents three specificities which need to be pointed out. In the first place, it is truly about a social and political revolution, born of, moreover, a long process of Westernization of the Muslim world and of decades of intellectual domination of the Left. But in contrast with the French and the Russian Revolutions, it explicitly adheres to a religious body;

[40] Marie Duboc, "Activism from the margins: overcoming the mobilization/demobilization dichotomy. A study of Left-Wing intellectuals in Egypt", unpublished article.

a discrepancy which does not emanate 'from the vision of the religious world of some particular social classes, but from the particular historical position of the religious intellectuals'.[41]

In the second place, it constitutes, with the French and the Russian Revolutions, one of the three 'model-revolutions' in human history, desirous of being popular and 'exportable'. In this sense, the revolution of 1979 not only marked the exit of Iran from the American fold without entering into that of the USSR, but it equally put a stop to the dependence of the Middle East with regard to the revolutionary models coming from elsewhere. But, a global event, in so far as it happened in front of the eyes of hundreds of thousands of television viewers, it redefined the universal, while narrowing it to the Muslim world alone. While facilitating this 'empowerment' in relation to the world-system, the Iranian experience was condemned to remain infinitely more radical than the other revolutionary experiences of the region, consequently arousing more expectations and eventually more disappointments than the others.

The third specificity of the Iranian Revolution has equally been double-edged: radical, yet profoundly conservative, it found its symbol in the old but dignified face of Khomeini, evidence of past sufferings and of authenticity, it based its sociological foundation on the clergy and the *bazari.* The 'revolution' appeared from then on as not the act of dissolution of a social and moral order but, on the contrary, as its restoration and reinforcement, which could only make a section of the middle classes or of liberal professions across the Middle East sympathetic to it. However, this social conservatism prevented the Sunni, Middle-Eastern youth from supporting it in the long-term.

However, this social conservatism prevented the Sunni, Middle-Eastern youth from supporting it in the long-term.

[41] Sami Zubaida, *Islam, the People and the State; Essays on Political Ideas and Movements in the Middle East,* London, I.B. Tauris, 1993, p. 80.

Born of a somber subjectivity, the tragedy of the Iranian Revolution, following its victory and through the course of the Iran-Iraq War is that it focuses on the cultural-religious question rather than the socio-political which was its principal trigger. It also redefines the stakes on a number of issues – from domination to alienation by the same yardstick.

The unfortunate comments of Michel Foucault, though an outstanding intellectual, and the response, implicit but fierce, of Maxime Rodinson[42] asking him to be more rational and more critical, enlighten us more than any other debate, on the foundations of 1979, in this cultural-religious context. That which Foucault finds novel and welcomes in this revolution is its linkages with religion and its unanimity which is not a hollow word devoid of meaning.

On the first point, he writes:

'Religion has truly been the vocabulary, the ceremonial, an eternal tragedy within which is lodged the historic drama of a people who consider their existence side by side with that of their sovereign'.

Fully aware that Islam was more than a religion, 'a way of life', 'belonging to a history and a civilization', he emphasizes that infact, the 'Islamic Movement (the Khomeinist Revolution) can burn down all religions, overthrow the most unstable regimes, and dismay the most sturdy ones. [43]

On the second point, he mentions specifically that all along 1979 'the absolute collective will' ceased to be an abstract principle: 'We have witnessed the collective will of the people in Teheran and throughout Iran. We should salute this since it does not occur every day'.[44]

[42] Maxime Rodinson, *L'Islam politique et croyance*, Paris, Fayard, 1993, pp. 261–95. For the background of this debate, see Yann Richard, op.cit. pp. 341–45.

[43] Michel Foucault, *Dits et écrits*, Paris, Gallimard, 1994, vol. 3, coll. "Nrf", pp. 746-47.

[44] Foucault is however outraged by the repression that rapidly rains upon the Liberals and Left organizations following the victory. See ibid., pp. 780–82.

In a sense Foucault was perfectly right, since these two elements have indeed been inseparable from the hope of collective freedom which manifested itself in 1979, and they radicalized it to the point of pushing tens of thousands of Iranians to voluntary self-sacrifice. However he did not understand that these two characteristics he greeted so enthusiastically were precisely those that led to the establishment of a highly conservative, disciplinarian and coercive social order, one that would subject the body to political and judicial authority as well as to male domination, or even convert it into a sacrificial site for a never-ending war. This opens the road to potential, millenarian interpretations of the world and its 'otherness', still relevant today after several decades.

This opens the road to potential, millenarian interpretations of the world and its 'otherness', still relevant today after several decades.

The Revolution of 1979 introduced a radical break with the political thought of the Middle East through the very manner of posing the question of alienation. It was not possible to get rid of alienation, either by the self-denial, extolled by the West[45], or with the construction of an universal through conflict, to bring an end to the dialectic of the master and the slave, as believed by the Left. Soul searching alone through a 'Biblical War' with a 'Master', led by soldiers and in face of an energy that is driven by sacrifice heretofore unseen in this world, can bring the alienation of the Muslim world to a close.

Moreover, building a government on earth of the 'Redeemers of Islam' or the clergy of Mahdi, could protect Muslims from descent into alienation and ignorance of divine guidance (Jahiliyya) preceding the promised return of the Messiah, the 'Guided One'.

A number of those whom we generically call the 'new Islamic thinkers' recall this period with a pang of sorrow, that the Muslim

[45] See *Djâlal al-e Ahmad*, L'occidentalite, Paris, L'Harmattan, 1988.

world has never been so estranged as when it thought it was finally emerging out of its isolation, thanks to Islam.

AFTER 1989

There is absolutely no doubt that the Iranian Revolution stood out as a model in the Middle East and outside in the Muslim world, at least in the 1980s. Yet it turned out to be 'difficult to reproduce' or to export. Not only has the passage to a revolution in the form of insurrections not been possible in the rest of the Muslim world but the articulation of the revolution with Shi'ite Messianism, centred on the martyrdom of Hussein, grandson of Mohammed and the hope of the return of the Mahdi, could not find a guarantor among the Sunnite militants. Likewise, the more Iran became a model because of the Revolution, the more it ceased being one because of the long war with Iraq. The war was for men from 1979 to 1980 the natural extension, the crowning, mystic and Messianic, of their revolution. On the other hand, within the Islamist opposition, again becoming powerful throughout 1979, it appears to be an immense waste of the power of Islam, not against a *taghuti* state or Israel, but very much against another Muslim country. Soon, without turning away from Iran, the *moujahid* fighters of the Arab world and elsewhere carried their military transhumance to another front, Afghanistan, where *jihad* was carried out against a power, exterior and atheist.

It is, however, on this second front that the future of the countries of the Middle East, of Islamism and of the revolutionary passions, reactivated by the events of 1979, will be decided. The countries will be capable of combining repression and tolerance towards the Islamists, transforming the revolutionary notables into orators[46] or doctorates and by recruiting the most radical

[46] Rémy Leveau, "Vers une function tribunicienne", in Serge Cordelier (ed.), *L'Islamisme*, Paris, La Découverte, 1994, pp. 57–65.

of them for the jihad in Afghanistan. Within Islamism, the most radical currents will emerge on this faraway terrain (just as in Pakistan, their home base), which will launch ten years later the Islamist guerrillas in Algeria and in Egypt, or will give birth to the radicalism of Al-Qaida. It is on Afghan soil, and not Iranian, that a true international Islamist will be born and the political vocabulary of Islamism will get a new direction by axiology. Gradually, volumes of commentaries of the Koran by Sayeed Qotb will give way to the Koran, codified and simplified, and reduced to a few verses of Al-Qaida.

Apart from Afghanistan and Sudan, – the two countries where the communist parties have been so strong in the past – the Islamists will not be able to attain power, either by war or by coup d'état, even less by revolution. However, Islamism as an ideology will be able to constitute a hegemonic counter-discourse to become the normalized, legitimate political syntax in a number of countries, from Egypt to Jordan or to Turkey in the 1980s. But the context of authoritarianism marking these countries will condemn it for being content with an oratorical posture, or consequently, for exposing itself to massive coercions.

The martyrdom of generations of Islamists will, therefore, take over from that of generations of the Left.

GLOSSARY

Asr-i-Saada: 'Age of happiness' from the prophecy of Muhammad
Asabiyya: social cohesion
Ba'ath: 'Resurrection', the only political party in Syria since 1966 and in Iraq between 1963 and 2003
Bazaris: people and traders in the market
Chehid: martyr
Chorech: 'revolution' (in Kurdish)
Dar al-harb: 'House of War', non-Muslim territory against which war is lawful

Dar al-Islam: 'House of Islam', territory which theoretically forbids resort to violence

Da'wa: call, by extension, ideology

GIGN: peacekeeping force of the national police

Fitna: discord, division, sedition

Ihtilal: revolution, coup d'État in Arabic and Turkish

Inquilab: revolution, reform in Arabic and Turkish

Intifada: uprising, upheaval, term used particularly in Palestine, but also in Iraq and Lebanon

Jahiliyya: ignorance, by extension, ignorance of the divine message

Kataib (Phalanges): Lebanese radical right party founded in 1936

Khurudj: exit, by extension, exit of the believers

Mahdi: The Messiah

Naqba: 'Disaster', term used to speak of the first Arab-Israel War of 1947–48

Taghut: Polytheism, by extension, reign of oppression

Tanzimat: 'Reorganization'; series of administrative reforms of large scale enterprises from the years, 1838–39 in the Ottoman Empire

Thawra: Revolution

Toudeh (Hezb-e Toudeh Iran): Party of the Iranian masses, founded in 1941

Umma: community of believers

Watbah: insurrection, term used particularly in Iraq in 1948

Zaim, zaama: chief, system based on the pre-eminence of the Chief

Front page of *The Tribune* announcing the executions of the revolutionaries, Bhagat Singh and Rajguru.

Source: 1931. http://en.wikipedia.org/wiki/Sukhdev_Thapar

POSTER-AFTER SAUNDERS' MURDER

"Notice"

By Hindustan Socialist Republic Army.

'Bureaucracy Beware'

With the death of J.P. Saunders the assassinaiton of Lala Lajpat Rai has been avenged.

It is a matter of great regret that a respected leader of 30 crores of people was attacked by an ordinary police officer like J.P. Saunders and met with his death at his mean hands. This national insul was a challenge to young men.

Today the world has seen that the people of India are not lifeless; their blood has not become cold. They can lay down their lives for the country's honour. The proof of this has been given by hte youth who are ridiculed and insulted by the leaders of their own country.

'Tyrant Government Beware'

Do not hurt the feelings of the oppressed suffering people of this country. Stop your devilish ways. Despite all your laws preventing us from keeping arms and despite all your watchfulness, people of this country would conitnue to get pistols and revolvers. Even if these arms are not adequae in numbers for an armed revolution, they would be sufficient for avenging the insult to the country's honour. Even if our own people condemn us and ridicule us and if foreign government subjects us to any amount of repression, we shall all be ever ready to teach a lesson to foreign tyrants who insult our national honour. Despite all opposition and repression, we shall carry forward the call for revolution and even we go to the scaffold for being hanged, we shall continue to shout:

"Long Live Revolution!"

We are sorry to have killed a man. But this man was a part of cruel, despicable and unjust system and killing him was a necessity. This man has been killed as an employ of the British Government. This Government is the most oppressive government in the world.

"We are sorry for shedding human blood but it becomes necessary to bathe he alter of Revolution with blood. Our aim is to bring about a revolution which would end all exploitation of man by man.

"Long live Revolution!"

Sd/- Balraj

18th December, 1928. Commander-in-Chief, HSRA

HSRA pamphlet after Saunder's murder, signed by Balraj, a pseudonym of Chandrashekhar Azad

Source: https://en.wikipedia.org/wiki/Bhagat_Singh#/media/File:Pamphlet_by_HSRA_after_Saunders_murder.jpg

chapter 4

The Making of Indian Revolutionaries (1885–1931)

Christophe Jaffrelot

> In spite of all my efforts, I could not find any revolutionary party that had clear ideas as to what they were fighting for, with the exception of the Ghadr Party which, having been inspired by the USA form of government, clearly stated that they wanted to replace the existing government by a republican form of government. All other parties consisted of men who had but one idea, i.e., to fight against the alien rulers. That idea is quite laudable but cannot be termed a revolutionary idea. We must make clear that revolution does not merely mean an upheaval or a sanguinary strife. Revolution necessarily implies the programme of systematic reconstruction of society on new and better adapted basis, after complete destruction of the existing state of affairs (i.e. regime). (Bhagat Singh, "Introduction" to Lala Ram Saran Das, *The Dreamland* cited in Shiv Verma (ed.), *Bhagat Singh. On the path to liberation*, Chennai, Bharati Puthakalayam, 2007, p. 96[1])

The keyword of the Indian political history is not revolution; it is *reform*, a word which, in the course of time, has been bracketed together with various epithets. The reform was, at first, religious when, from the beginning of the 19th century, in the face of propaganda by Christian missionaries, enlightened

[1] For an online version, see https://www.marxists.org/archive/bhagat-singh/x01/x01/x01.htm

Brahmins endeavoured to modernize Hinduism – claiming to restore its original purity to give it a quasi-monotheistic version. Later the reform became social when the movements committed to religious reforms took note of how the social and the religious, weighed down by the caste system, were inextricably related in Hinduism. All along the 19th century,[2] one hears of 'socio-religious reform' to denote mainly the groups which mobilized themselves for the cause of the untouchables and women. Finally, the reform was political. The British, initiated it after they, in a sense, reproduced in India the same model that they had tried out in their own country while democratizing the form of government at regular intervals: in 1882, the Self-Government Act created partly elective Councils in towns and districts; in 1909, the provincial Legislative Councils were significantly upgraded; in 1919, these bodies acquired more power, giving the provinces a form of colonial parliamentarianism; and finally in 1935, the Government of India Act – from which the Indian Constitution of 1950 will derive many of its provisions – was one more step in the same direction.

After 1947, 'the world's largest democracy' has continued to reform itself by integrating in the political game subaltern groups which, till then, were sidelined. Lower castes and even Dalits entered into the system thanks to positive discrimination schemes, which had been introduced by the British and improved under Nehru.[3] B.R. Ambedkar, the most famous Dalit leader, played a role in this process before and after independence. Not a revolutionary in the classic sense of the word, he campaigned for the respect of human rights by legal and political means, rejecting violence. He not only played a major role in the drafting of the

[2] Kenneth Jones, *Socio-religious Reform Movements in British India*, Cambridge, Cambridge University Press, 1989.

[3] Christophe Jaffrelot, *India's Silent Revolution – The Rise of the Lower Castes in North India*, New York/Columbia University Press; London/Hurst; New Delhi/Permanent Black, 2003.

Indian Constitution, but created political parties which fought elections from the 1930s onwards.[4]

Does it mean that there is no revolutionary in India? Certainly not. Firstly, many reformists claimed that they were revolutionaries.[5] It was the case with the disciples of Gandhi who considered that the non-violent path of the Mahatma, so radically idealist, was a revolutionary way to bring about a rupture with the political and social institutions. From here emerged in the 1970s the movement for 'Total Revolution' initiated by Jaya Prakash Narayan. 'JP' fought in a peaceful way Indira Gandhi's authoritarianism, and was largely responsible for defeating her by bringing the opposition on a common platform.[6] But Gandhism does not qualify as a proper revolutionary movement. First, the Mahatma never questioned either the importance of private property as the means of production or the caste system which he wished would be rid of its hierarchical aspects, one of them being Untouchability.[7]

Secondly, and more importantly, there are other political activists known as 'Revolutionaries' in the history of India – at least from the late 19th century onwards, when the very idea of revolution was associated with that of anti-British militancy. However, their worldview owed a lot to Hindu traditions and European anarchism, as we will see in the first part of this Chapter. In the second part, we

[4] Christophe Jaffrelot, *Dr Ambedkar and Untouchability. Analysing and Fighting Caste,* New York/Columbia University Press; London/Hurst; New Delhi/ Permanent Black, 2004. Similarly the Communists enrolled themselves in the electoral process since the election of 1951–52, the first in independent India.

[5] See, for example, Mathew Zachariah, *Revolution through Reform. A comparison of Sarvodaya and Conscientization*, New Delhi, Vistaar Publications, 1988 and Geoffrey Ostergaard, *Nonviolent Revolution in India*, New Delhi, Gandhi Peace Foundation, 1985.

[6] Vasant Nargolkar, *JP's Crusade for Revolution*, New Delhi, S. Chand, 1975.

[7] Dennis Dalton, 'The Gandhian View of Caste and Caste after Gandhi', in Philip Mason (ed.) *India and Ceylon: Unity and Diversity*, London-New York, Oxford University Press, 1967.

will show that, by the 1910s–1920s, revolution in India gradually came to signify the same as elsewhere, after republicanism and socialism became widespread ideologies. The years 1920s–1930s thus marked the secularization of the revolutionary movement, which therefore found justifications other than religious for its violent techniques. But this movement did not entirely accept violence and continued to hold on to some specific traits of its origin – notably the glorification of individual sacrifice and the path of martyrdom – at the expense of a heightened sense of organization.

'TERRO-HINDUISM', THE INDIAN VERSION OF ANARCHISM (1885–1914)

From the end of the 19th century to World War I, British India became the theatre of a revolutionary movement, marked, at the same time, by the cult of individual violence and the influence of Hindu religion. In fact, anti-colonial struggle was seen as a sacred cause for which recourse to violence was justified by certain traits of Hinduism. This political culture was particularly popular in Bengal and Maharashtra.

Maharashtra and Bengal: Crucibles of a Political Culture of Violence

In 1885, the Indian National Congress was born with the coming together of members of the Indian elite who were mostly preoccupied to lobby the British in order to improve their position in the state apparatus. The Congress' presence was particularly strong in two provinces where the administration and the Universities set up by the British were among the oldest: Bengal – where Calcutta served as the capital of the Raj till 1911 – and the Bombay Presidency. In these two regions, parallel to the crystallization of a school of thought known as the 'Moderates' in the Congress, after 1895 developed an 'Extremist' current that readily legitimized anti-British violence.

In Maharashtra, those who belonged to this milieu rallied behind a leader, Bal Gangadhar Tilak, whose radical discourse was replete with Hindu references. Tilak drew some of his inspiration from the Bhagavad Gita, a key text of Hinduism enshrined in the *Mahabharata,* the epic that narrates the main battle of two clans belonging to the same family – the Kauravas and the Pandavas (the latter being guided by Lord Krishna himself). For Tilak, the Gita justified the recourse to violence in politics.[8] Refuting the classical interpretations of the text which emphasize quests of knowledge and devotion, he revisited the Yoga of action (Karma Yoga). He found in it the essence of the core passage of the Gita, the sermon of Krishna to Arjuna, the leader of the Pandavas[9] in which the former explains that each and every act, even if it is violent, is legitimate if it is undertaken for the good of the world and in a spirit of renouncement – without any expectation of rewards.

This interpretation is one-sided because, in fact, Krishna requested Arjuna to resort to violence against his own cousins, the Kauravas, not only to defend the socio-cosmic order in a spirit of renouncement, but also – and primarily – to assume his Kshatriyahood. It is because he belonged to the order of the Kshatriya (the warrior caste) that Arjun is called upon to take recourse to violence by Krishna[10]: it is his dharma. Tilak interpreted rather loosely the message of Krishna to Arjuna, as if

[8] The first edition of his book, *The Secret of the Gita*, in Marathi, which appeared in 1915, is a compilation of articles and speeches written way back in 1902. One will get an idea of the influence of this work, while going through the list of publications in other Indian languages, which figures on page 5 of the first edition in English, where only the title was in Marathi. See B.G.Tilak, *Srimad Bhagavadgita Rahasya*, Poona, Tilak Bros., 1936.

[9] B. G. Tilak, *Srimad Bhagavadgita Rahasya or Karma Yoga Shastra*, Poona, 1965, p. 424, 478 and 645.

[10] Madeleine Biardeau emphasizes that for a Kshatriya, the accomplishment of his duty, which necessitated violence, is itself the condition of his salvation. (M.Biardeau, 'Introduction', *The Mahabharata*, Paris, Garnier Flammarion, 1985, vol. 1, p. 37.)

it was addressed to all men (and not only to the Kshatriyas) and as if it was intended to save the nation (and not the socio-cosmic order or Dharma).[11] That Tilak makes clever use of a sacred theme with a political end in mind is confirmed by the way he instrumentalized other identity symbols. He thus initiated the cult of Shivaji – the chief of the Maratha confederation in the 18th century –, who killed the emissary of his enemy, the emperor Aurangzeb, who had come to negotiate on his invitation. Tilak justified this act by invoking the Gita again: 'Did Shivaji commit a sin in killing Afzul Khan? The answer to this question can be found in the *Mahabharata* itself. The Divine Krishna teaching in the Gita tells us that we may kill even our teachers and our kinsmen and no blame attaches if we are not actuated by selfish desires. Shivaji did nothing from a desire to fill his own belly. It was in a praiseworthy object that he murdered Afzul Khan for the good of others'.[12]

In Bengal, the ideologue who inspired the first revolutionaries in the same way as Tilak did in Maharashtra but who, undoubtedly, took a more active part than him in their fight against the British was Aurobindo Ghose.[13] He was probably the most Westernized of all the revolutionaries of his generation. Born in 1872, he was sent to England for his studies when he was just eleven years old and it was there that he became a nationalist. He even joined a secret society, 'Lotus and Dagger', set up by Indian students in London. Having narrowly missed the entrance examination of the Indian Civil Service, Aurobindo returned to India in 1893 without knowing any of the Indian languages but with a vast knowledge of revolution that he had acquired in Europe. He thus rejected the

[11] Minoo Adenwalla, 'Hindu concepts and the Gita in early Indian thought', in Robert K. Sakai (ed.) *Studies in Asia*, Lincoln, University of Nebraska Press, 1961.

[12] Cited in Valentine Chirol, *Indian Unrest,* London, Macmillan, 1910, p. 46.

[13] He is rightly described as 'the philosopher of the revolution' by Haridas and Uma Mukherjee ('The alleged uniqueness of India's freedom movement', *Modern Review*, no. 112, 1962, pp. 106–07).

reformist model – referred to in the introduction – of the British reformers who, in his eyes, had been able to bring about less change to the country in seven centuries than the French Revolution. For him, France gained freedom 'not through any decent and orderly expansion, but through a purification by blood and fire'.[14] While working in the administration of the princely state of Baroda, in the West of India, the gateway to the Presidency of Bombay, he became a member of a secret society of Tilakist[15] allegiance.

In his mature writings he will, anyway, legitimize recourse to violence in politics as Tilak did. He thus considered that 'The *Gita* is the best answer to those who shrink from battle as sin and aggression as a lowering of morality ... Aggression is unjust only when unprovoked, violence unrighteousness when used wantonly or for unrighteous ends'.[16]

Aurobindo was, however, a thinker more sophisticated than Tilak. First, he was not content with the religiosity of the masses for the purpose of political mobilization, as did Tilak during the Ganesh festivals he initiated. Furthermore, he considered religion as the foundation of the superior identity of India in an inspirational ethno-nationalist vein. Second, he did not look at violence as an end in itself, but was looking for a way to make it useful, that is to say, revolutionary – unlike the Tilakites.[17] He

[14] Peter Heehs, 'Foreign influences on Bengali revolutionary terrorism', *Modern Asian Studies*, 28(3), 1994, reproduced in Peter Heehs, *Nationalism, Terrorism, Communalism. Essays in Modern Indian History*, Delhi-New York, Oxford University Press, 1998, p. 70.

[15] K.R. Srinivasa Iyengar, *Sri Aurobindo: A Biography and a History*, Pondichéry, Sri Aurobindo Ashram/SABDA, 4th revised and enlarged ed.

[16] Cited by Peter Heehs, 'Aurobindo Ghose and revolutionary terrorism', *South Asia*, 15(2), 1992, reproduced in P. Heehs, *Nationalism, Terrorism, Communalism*, *op.cit.*, p. 55. See also an article 'The Age of the Gita again in India', in *Jugantar*, the journal of Aurobindo's brother Barindra, as reprinted by Valentine Chirol among others (*op.cit.* p. 91).

[17] In 1918 Aurobindo will write a highly eulogistic preface to a collection of lectures given by Tilak where he subtly differentiates himself from his so-called

thus wished to create 'volunteer forces which would be the nucleus of an army of open revolt'.[18] But he was at the same time aware of the necessity of leading and carrying out a clandestine action and in 1902 sent Jatindra Nath Banerjee, one of the bodyguards of the Maharaja of Baroda, to Bengal to set up a gymnastic club. This, he thought, would make the youth of Calcutta physically and morally strong. He would follow him in 1906 to work in the Bengal National College and continue the career of a public intellectual with extremist political leanings. He will thus support the setting up of secret societies for carrying out violent actions.

Revolutionaries as Individuals in the Quest of Self-esteem

Terrorist violence towards the British was initially the act of isolated individuals influenced by the speeches of the Extremists. The Chapekar brothers in Maharashtra were a case in point. They were inspired by Tilak who, on 12 May 1897 wrote in his newspaper, *The Kesari*: 'All the sensible men of today seem to agree on the origins of the party of the bomb. The party of the bomb is born of oppression, unleashed by the class of officials'.[19] Ten days later, the Chapekar brothers executed two British officials who were fighting against an epidemic of plague when they entered homes in a brutal manner without respecting the privacy of Indian family life. They were arrested and condemned to death while Tilak was imprisoned for eighteen months. If what the Chapekar brothers did was an isolated act, it definitely motivated others to take up terrorism as

mentor: 'It is equally a mistake to think [of] Mr. Tilak as by nature a revolutionary leader; that is not his character or his political temperament. The Indian people, generally, with the possible exception of emotional and idealistic [people] and Bengal have nothing or very little of the revolutionary temper; they can be goaded to revolution like and every people on the face of earth, but naturally they are conservative in temperament and deliberate in action'. (Sri Aurobindo, *Bankim, Tilak, Dayanand*, Delhi, Sarvadeshik Arya Pratinidhi Sabha, 1984 [1909], p. 19).

[18] *Ibid.*, p. 60.

[19] Cited by H.M. Ghodke, *Revolutionary Nationalism in Western India*, New Delhi, Classical Publishing House, 1990, p. 33.

a vocation.[20] At the turn of the 20th century the revolutionaries of Maharashtra and Bengal, though they developed some direct contacts, moved in that direction in a parallel way. They emulated the European anarchists through their individual actions while finding equivalents to their modus operandi in the Hindu religion.

Tilak, Savarkar and the 'Hinduization' of Anarchism

In Maharashtra, the Savarkar brothers played a pioneering role in the vernacularization of European techniques of individual violence. Their father, a small landowner and money-lender in a village of Nasik district, belonged to the same clan as Tilak and was an admirer of his nationalism. He taught his three sons – Ganesh, the eldest, Vinayak, the second, and Narayan, the youngest, the glorious history of the Mahrattas when he used to read out to them from *The Kesari*. Of the three, Vinayak was the most politically inclined. After his admission to the high school in Nasik, in 1900, he founded a secret society, Mitra Mela (The Friends' Festival) which was primarily engaged in organizing Tilak's versions of festivals in honor of Ganesh and Shivaji.

From 1902 onwards, while still a student of Ferguson College in Pune, he hardened the rules of admission to Mitra Mela, whose members had now to take a vow to sacrifice their lives for the cause of the Indian nation. In 1905, armed with a B.A. degree, he left for Bombay and transformed the Mitra Mela into the Abhinav Bharat Society (The Society of Young India). In this he was directly inspired by the young Italy of Mazzini, but also by the methods of the Russian nihilists. Savarkar was, moreover, the first to introduce in India a book called *Secret Societies of the European Revolution 1776–1876* by Thomas Frost which he wanted the Indians to emulate. In 1906, Savarkar decided to go to Europe to learn more techniques and postulated – with a letter of recommendation from Tilak – at the India House that

[20] On the dimension, more traditionalist than nationalist, of the heroic feats of the Chapekar brothers, see *ibid*. p. 84.

S.K. Varma had just established in London to provide shelter to Indian students[21]. There soon developed a relationship between him, the Russian terrorists and the militants of the Sinn Fein for a better understanding of their techniques. Two emissaries of Savarkar – Hemchandra Das and Senapati Bapat – thus obtained from an old Russian nihilist, then a refugee in Paris, a manual on the making of explosives.

While Savarkar was exposed to foreign influences during his trip to Europe, he continued to combine his violent nationalism with Hinduism. When the elder of the Chapekar brothers was given the death sentence in 1898, Savarkar vowed to take revenge by sacrificing his body and soul for the liberation of India in front of the goddess Ashtabhuja, a form of Durga. Making sacred a political commitment by taking a religious vow, was, at that time, the norm among Indian revolutionaries, mostly Hindus. One of the mainstays of Hinduism – sacrifice – is omnipresent in the nationalist discourse of Savarkar and other revolutionaries. In 1909, while writing on the revolt of the sepoys of 1857 – which he called the first war of independence' of India – he described this political battle in religious terms to make it 'the great sacrifice':

> While the date of this National Vengeance is approaching nearer and yet nearer, it is but proper that the requisite sacrifice should be offered to the sacred and terrible God of Fire, the Lord of us all, so that the presiding deity of this grand work may be propitiated [...] This presiding Goddess of National Anger is rising from the Yajna Kunda [the site of sacrifice] with all her limbs! What a terrible fierceness! Be propitious, O Goddess, be propitious! We offer the perfect offering of our presiding deity herself in order that thou mayest be propitious. Accept this offering, which we are going to offer! All the cartridges that can be found in the

[21] On S.K. Varma and India House, see Indulal Yagnik, *Shyamaji Krishnavarma. Life and Times of an Indian Revolutionary*, Bombay, Lakshmi Publications, 1950 and Harald Fisher-Tiné, *Shyamji Krishnavarma. Sanskrit, Sociology and Anti-Imperialism*, London, Routledge, 2014.

> Dum Dum [a town of Bengal] factory, dip them, cook them, in cows' and pigs' blood,[22] bring them as a complete offering for the presiding Goddess of the Sacrifice, and – bring them quick![23]

Savarkar narrates here a historical event using the idiom of the Hindu imagination, with a lyricism that recalls the poems of his childhood. Beyond what could only be an exercise once more in vernacularization with the purpose of political communication, Savarkar himself saw terrorist activity as religious sacrifice. In 1909, his brother Ganesh, whom he had put in charge of Abhinav Bharat before leaving for London, was given life imprisonment and sent to the Andaman Islands for seditious writings. Vinayak then decided to get Curzon Wyllie, one of the advisors to the Secretary of the State of India, assassinated. Hounded, once the crime was committed, Savarkar took refuge in Paris before coming back to London where he knowingly threw himself into imminent danger for his participation in 'national sacrifice'. The religious nature of this sacrifice – in his view – is clear from the letter he wrote a little later to Ganesh's wife, whom he likened to the Mother Goddess:

> ... and now here I am, O Mother, bound to Thy Sacrificial Pillar! What of These! Had we been seven instead of only three [brothers] I would have Sacrificed them all – in thy cause. Thy cause is Holy! Thy Cause I believed to be the Cause of God and in serving it I knew I served the Lord!.

Sent to prison in the Andaman Islands, Savarkar will become a Hindu nationalist, more anti-Muslim than anti-British. When he will be freed in 1937, he will be made the President of the Hindu Mahasabha, a party known for its militant Hindu politics.

[22] Allusion to the element of provocation of the Sepoys in the Indian army. They revolted against the introduction of the cartridges, greased with the fat of the cow and pig – which was sacrilegious to the Hindus and the Muslims respectively.

[23] An Indian Nationalist, *The Indian War of Independence of 1857*, no place of publication, no publisher, 1909, p. 56 and p. 58.

The Terro-Heroism of the Worshippers of the Goddess in Bengal

In Bengal, the first secret society, the Anushilan Samiti, was born in 1902 by fusing together the gymnastic club of Jatindranath (the friend of Aurobindo who had come from Baroda) and another of Pramatha Nath Mitra. The primary aim of these men was to inculcate a sense of physical and mental discipline (Anushilan) among the students of Calcutta, the principal base of the organization being an *akhara*[24] in the northern part of the city. Aurobindo's brother, Barindra Kumar, joined this place, temporarily in 1903, then permanently in 1905 and introduced there an inclination towards violent action. In 1906, Barindra started *Jugantar*, a weekly newspaper whose circulation soared to 50,000 copies in 1908[25], a sign of the popularity of the revolutionaries in Bengal after the mass mobilization of the Swadeshi movement.[26]

The objective of the Anushilan Samiti was the independence of India at any cost. In the third issue of *Jugantar*, Aurobindo Ghosh, who was its mentor[27], published an article titled "Our Political Ideal" where he wrote: 'independence [swadhinata] in our

[24] The *akharas*, places of physical exercises associated with Hindu temples, started growing in number at the end of the 19th century, especially in Maharashtra and in Bengal. In the latter province especially, they were reactions to the stereotype of the Indians, (especially the Bengali), the natives, who the British looked upon as weak and effeminate. See John Rosselli, 'The self-image of effeteness: physical education and nationalism in nineteenth century Bengal', *Past and Present,* 86, 1980.

[25] James Campbell Ker, *Political Trouble in India 1907–1917*, Calcutta, 1973 [1917], p. 62.

[26] In reaction to the partition of Bengal into two, the Swadeshi Movement had been launched in 1905 by the Extremists in the Congress.

[27] The extent to which Aurobindo was implicated in the terrorist organizations of Bengal is the subject of endless historiographic debate. One can, without any doubt, believe his brother when he says that Aurobindo was their 'motivator' (Peter Heehs, 'Aurobindo Ghose', *op.cit.*, p. 45.)

educational, commercial and political life has to be attained by any means possible'[28]. Terrorist action was therefore perceived by the members of the Anushilan Samiti and of one of its offshoots, the Maniktala group[29] – whose major driving force was Barindra Ghosh – as a political lever for nationalist causes. From 1906 onwards, Barindra started making bombs on a small scale. The following year, one of the members of the Maniktala group, Hemchandra Das, along with Senapati Bapat, went to Europe to learn – as mentioned above – the art of making bombs from a Russian anarchist, Nicholas Safranski. Between 1906 and 1908, the Maniktala group targeted three British dignitaries – Bampfylde Fuller (Lt. Governor of East Bengal), Andrew Fraser (Lt. Governor of West Bengal), Douglas Kingsford (district judge of Muzaffarpur), whom the group tried to assassinate, but in vain. Finally, a young member of this group, Khudiram Bose, killed by mistake two English women – Mrs Kennedy and her daughter – in Muzaffarpur, while the person they had targeted was Kingsford.[30] The reaction of the British was immediate and the crackdown resulted in the arrest of the Ghosh brothers and the breaking up of their network in what came to be known as the Alipore bomb case, after the name of the prison where the trial took place.

* * *

The discipline of the Anushilan Samiti was entirely religious, at least apparently. The movement followed codes inspired

[28] Cited by Peter Heehs, 'The Maniktala Secret Society', in P. Heehs, *Nationalism, Terrorism, Communalism*, op. cit., p. 15.

[29] Named after a locality in Calcutta where it had its headquarters.

[30] This officer, in charge of the administration of the Bengal Presidency, was behind the extreme ruthlessness of the British in the province, as evident in the harshness with which he had reacted to an article of Bhupendra Nath Dutt (brother of the great Hindu reformer, Swami Vivekananda), who was sentenced to imprisonment for one year.

by ascetic orders of warrior-monks, as described by Bankim Chandra Chatterjee, the first Bengali novelist, in his major work, *Anandamath* (the Abbey of Bliss)[31]. The religious dimension of the movement became apparent to its members at the initiation ceremony itself, when the new entrant took pledge, facing Kali, with the *Bhagavad Gita* in one hand and a revolver in the other, the presence of the goddess reminding here of what the organization, in its use of violence, owed to the Shakta sects (worshippers of the Goddess – known as Kali or Durga). Moreover, the structure of the Anushilan Samiti reflected one of the key concepts of the Hindu sects, the *guru/sishya* (master/ disciple) relationship, where the disciple must offer his complete loyalty, devotion and respect to his master. This ethos is at the heart of Bankim's seminal novel which narrates the fight for the Mother-Goddess (identified somewhere as Kali, somewhere else as the cow looked upon as foster mother and sacred) to 'the community of the Sons' forming 'a sect of worshippers' under the authority of the guru.[32] As ascetic (*sannyasin*) fighters they renounced the world (which is temporary anyway) "to cultivate these qualities" which make the English so strong, and in particular to learn the art of war. At the time of their initiation into the Anushilan Samiti they dissociated themselves from an exterior circle, abandoning their family and blurring the social distinctions arising from the caste system.[33]

In the early years of the 20th century, a large number of Bengali newspapers claiming to adhere to "extremism" peppered

[31] See France Bhattacharya, *Les intellectuels bengalis et l'impérialisme britannique*, Paris, Collège de France, 2010, pp. 203 – 314.

[32] The title of the song *Vande Mataram* (Hail! Oh Mother!) of the ascetic fighters described by Bankim will be used by Aurobindo for the name of his review published from Calcutta from 1906 onwards.

[33] Bankim Chandra Chatterjee, *Le Monastère de la félicité*, Paris, Presses Orientalistes de France, 1985, introduced and translated by France Bhattacharya. It is to be noted that Jitendranath Banerjee will leave Anushilan Samiti in 1904 to become a *sannyasin*.

their articles with references to Shakti, the divine energy of the Goddess who put her worshippers against the demons – the British – from whom it was their duty to free the country.[34] After 1905, the Hindu dimension of the secret societies of Bengal was strengthened by the Swadeshi movement whose architects strove hard to mobilize the masses on the basis of a religious symbolism. The riots between Hindus and Muslims which took place in the second half of the decade further complicated the relation between the two communities, certain secret societies severing all ties with the Muslims. *Jugantar* wrote: 'Favoured sons of independence, Musalmans, be warned! [...] The Hindus are certain to be independent. Will Musalmans then allow themselves to remain without that nectar?'[35] These words reflected the suspicion that started to weigh on the Muslims, accused of looking for protection from the British, rather than fighting against them. Had not the Muslim League, founded in 1906, just demanded a separate electorate for the Muslim minority?

The interrogatories of the 36 accused in the Alipore bomb case helps us to identify the religious as well as political nature of their motivations. These young men, most of them from the upper castes, mention the importance of the Hindu writings during their training to become apprentice – revolutionaries. If some of them do not provide more detailed information,[36] others cite the Upanishads[37] and another large number, the Gita.[38] One of them even indicated that he had been in two minds: whether to become a *sannyasin* or a revolutionary?[39]

[34] Valentine Chirol offers an authentic compilation in his book taken from his reporting, which appeared in *The Times* of London, *Indian Unrest*, op.cit. pp. 18–19.

[35] Cited by Peter Heehs, op.cit., pp. 17–18.

[36] Noorul Hoda, *The Alipore bomb case. A historic pre-independence trial*, New Delhi, Niyogi Books, 2008, p. 78 and 90.

[37] Ibid., p. 87, 95 and 103.

[38] Ibid., p. 88, 95 and 103.

[39] Ibid., p. 97.

Thus, at the turn of the 20th century, the nascent revolutionary movement of India is marked by two major features in its two bastions, Maharashtra and Bengal: the cult of violence and some religious inspiration.[40] Five lessons can be drawn from here:

1) The Indian case teaches us that there are quite a few ways of becoming a revolutionary. In the Hindu milieu, what defines subversion the best – in the sense of a revolt not only social but also moral – is possibly recourse to violence. Not that the Hindu society had ignored violence. In fact, this is the repertoire of the Kshatriyas *par excellence*. But this caste group is absent from Bengal and Maharashtra and conflicts associated with the Brahmins – the caste group from where most of the revolutionaries of these regions came – did not express themselves *ideally* in a violent manner.[41] Formerly, traditionally, a money-lender, to recover the payment of a debt, kept standing in front of the residence of his debtor to

[40] It would remain incomplete if one does not cite Punjab where assimilation of the revolutionary movement with the Hindu community was reinforced during 1900 by the activism of the Arya Samaj – a movement of socio-religious reform, influenced by militant Hinduism. In 1907, the Punjabis from the rural areas responded by agitating violently against the law, making more difficult the conditions of exploitation of zones open to agriculture since 1887, following an active policy of irrigation. It became more difficult for those living in the cities – the Hindu majority – to buy land from the peasants – predominantly Muslims – even when the latter were indebted to the former (which was frequent) and had no other way of returning the cash. This policy of trying to protect the 'agrarian tribes', from which the British took support, angered the Arya Samajists, of whom there were many among the urban intelligentsia. Their demonstrations and violent acts were met with severe repression on the part of the British. Lajpat Rai and Ajit Singh, the leaders of a local terrorist organization, were consequently deported to Mandalay in Burma.

[41] Talking of the situation of the princely state of Sirohi in Rajasthan, Denis Vidal writes that one could 'classify the castes and the communities of the kingdom according to their traditional attitude towards violence.'(D. Vidal, *Violences et vérités. Un royaume du Rajasthan face au pouvoir colonial,* Paris, Éditions de l'EHESS, 1995, pp. 24–25.)

undertake a fast rather than resorting to strong-arm tactics,[42] the moral pressure exerted by his sacrifice being the only violence compatible with his status. For the Brahmin, and a great many, who tried to imitate him, violence was a taboo which, in fact, could only lead to a form of moral decay[43]. Resorting to it, for the terrorists of the 1890s, was an act of transgression stronger than in other societies.[44]

2) This transgression was, without any doubt, easier to carry out for Brahmins in the two above-mentioned regions, Maharashtra and Bengal[45]. In Bengal, the religious culture associated with the Shakti cult, certainly produced a ground more favorable than elsewhere[46] – all the more so since these local traditions

[42] On this point, see Charles Malamoud, 'Le jeûne du créancier', *in* Louis Renou (ed.), *L'Inde fondamentale*, Paris, Hermann, 1978, pp. 164–74.

[43] See Charles Malamoud, 'Remarks on Dissuasion in Ancient India', in D. Vidal, G. Tarabout and E. Meyer (eds.), *Violence/Non-Violence. Some Hindu Perspectives*, Delhi, Manohar, 2003, p. 216.

[44] The nuance is important: no society gives the first place to violence, as it puts it in great danger; but in Hinduism, violence is less legitimate than in most other societies.

[45] Maharashtra and Bengal were the two strongholds of the terrorist movement. It cannot, however, be said that one learnt about revolution from the other even if they maintained relations from the beginning. In addition to the contacts already mentioned, in Europe, between Savarkar, Hemchandra Das and Bapat, one can cite here the on-off relationship between the revolutionaries of Western India and the Bengalis. Apart from the state of Baroda, where Aurobindo worked (see Peter Heehs op. cit., p. 24), the Central Provinces sent apprentice – terrorists to Bengal like Keshav Baliram Hedgewar, the founder of the Rashtriya Swayamsevak Sangh (RSS) who left Nagpur for sometime in order to get into the inner circle of the Anushilan Samiti in Calcutta. But it cannot be said that Bengal had assimilated violent action from Maharashtra. If anti-British attitudes found expression in violent action at an early date, Bengal was able to quickly catch up. Furthermore, Tilak hailed the assassination attempt in Muzaffarpur in such eulogizing terms that he was sentenced to imprisonment in Mandalay for six years.

[46] In this context Valentine Chirol cites a call to patriotic sacrifice which would not have meant the same to people other than the Bengalis to whom it is

and customs had already allowed the Brahmins not to adhere to strict vegetarianism, a major exception given the importance of diet in the hierarchy of castes. In Maharashtra, where there was no Kshatriya caste either, their role was taken up by Brahmins, and in particular by Chitpavans. In the 17th century, they had not only become administrators of the kingdom founded by Shivaji but also his generals[47]. And this had fostered a martial ethos atypical of the brahminical milieu. This culture of war, without doubt, contributed to the penchant for the bomb, demonstrated by the supporters of political violence whose architects – from Tilak to Savarkar and the Chapekar brothers – all belonged to the miniscule but very influential caste of the Chitpavans.[48]

---

addressed: 'Will the Bengali worshippers of Shakti shrink from the shedding of blood? The number of Englishmen in this country is not above one lakh and a half, and what is the number of English officials in each district? If you are firm in your resolution you can in a single day bring English rule to an end. Lay down your life, but first take a life. The worship of the goddess will not be consummated if you sacrifice your lives at the shrine of independence without shedding blood'. (V. Chirol, op. cit., p. 94).

[47] On the Chitpavan Brahmins and their martial ethos, see G. Johnson, 'Chitpavan. Brahmins and Politics in Western India in the Late Nineteenth and Early Twentieth Centuries', in E. Leach and S.N. Mukherjee (eds.), *Elites in South Asia*, Cambridge, Cambridge University Press, 1970, p. 100 and M. Patterson, 'Chitpavan Brahman Family Histories; sources for a study of social structures and social change in Maharashtra', in M. Singer and B. Cohn (eds), *Structure and Change in Indian Society*, Jaipur, Rawat, 1996 [1968], p. 403.

[48] However, Asish Nandy's culturalist assumption suggesting a unilateral relationship between Chitpavan Brahmins and militant nationalism needs to be qualified: if most of the Maharashtrian terrorists and Hindu nationalist leaders were Chitpavans, many Chitpavans joined other political schools of thought. On this issue see C. Jaffrelot, 'Opposing Gandhi: Hindu Nationalism and Political Violence', in Denis Vidal, Gilles Tarabout & Eric Meyer (eds.), *Violence/Non-Violence. Some Hindu Perspectives*, Delhi, Manohar, 2003, pp. 299–324.

3) The fact that resorting to violence was easier in Bengal and Maharashtra than elsewhere, does not mean that violence was necessarily an end in itself for most of the revolutionaries. Certainly, some were content with throwing bombs to affirm their penchant for subversion. But others had quite different motives:

– vengeance: the action of the Chapekar brothers or that of Madanlal Dhingra, the assassin of Curzon-Wyllie, are cases in point. Most of the targeted assassinations aimed at judges who had meted out heavy punishment on Indians. Generally speaking, 'the terrorists were moved by a strong desire, very common among them, to retaliate the brutality of the police and the arrogance of the officials'.[49] This desire of taking vengeance will only become more and more intense as the perpetrators of the assassination attempts are arrested and tortured with more intense savagery.

– regaining self-esteem: while the Indians were subjected to the colonial yoke, the murder of one of their 'masters' contributed to free themselves from an inferiority complex, at times, obsidian[50], by showing the vulnerability of the dominant. In this context, violence is, as Franz Fanon, says in *The Wretched of the Earth*, 'a cleansing force'; 'It frees the native from his inferiority complex and from its despair and inaction; it makes him fearless and restores his self-respect'.[51]

– the exemplary nature of sacrifice: the signs of courage, of which the assassination attempts are witnesses, are all the more great as the assassins are often fully aware of the risks

[49] Peter Heehs, "Terrorism and the national movement', *The Historian*, 55, 3 (1993), reproduced *in* P. Heehs, *Nationalism, terrorism, communalism,* op.cit, p. 5.

[50] See J. Rosselli, 'The self-image of effeteness: physical education and nationalism in nineteenth century Bengal', *op. cit.*.

[51] Frantz Fanon, *The Wretched of the Earth*, New York, Grove Press, 2004 (1963), p. 51.

run. They are indeed spoken of in terms of sacrifice, a vocation worthy of emulation. To dare to kill and to go to the gallows without being least afraid of death is most prestigious. This, for the revolutionaries, was a way of arousing people to adhere to the cause of the noble and heroic deeds. The assassin of the Kennedys, the mother and the daughter, Khudiram Bose, who missed his target and killed two women, became a hero in Bengal: in Calcutta, people were desperate to get hold of his photograph and a number of young men carried his name stitched on the lapels of their clothes.[52] As for the assassin of the Indian traitor who had betrayed his accomplices, his body was taken in procession to the funeral pyre by a veritable sea of people.[53] The approach of the Indian revolutionaries here resembles the 'propaganda by action' (a phrase coming from the formula coined by the French anarchists,'La propagande par le fait') of the European anarchists.

4) The importance of foreign influences constitutes precisely the penultimate conclusion one can draw at this stage. The educated Indian elite had been familiar, since long, with European political movements. Between 1879 and 1889, Y. Vidyabhushan published in Bengal a biography of Mazzini and a quarter of a century later,[54] one of Garibaldi. Meanwhile, Savarkar and Lajpat Rai brought out their own separate biographies of Mazzini. They were also familiar with the actions of quite a few other nationalists who did not hesitate to take recourse to violence (as Kossuth). They were, above all, particularly well-informed of the techniques of the European secret societies. Thomas Frost's *The Secret Societies of the European*

[52] Valentine Chirol, op.cit., p. 97.

[53] I. Mallikarjuna Sharma, op.cit., p. 53.

[54] Peter Heehs, 'Foreign influences on Bengali revolutionary terrorism', *Modern Asian Studies*, 28(3), 1994; reproduced in Peter Heehs, *Nationalism, terrorism, communalism*, op.cit, p. 69.

Revolution 1776–1876, published in London in 1876, taught them the modus operandi of the Italian and Irish Nationalists – particularly the Fenians and the Russian Nihilists whose organization of watertight cells had often impressed them. Further, their stay in Europe familiarized them with European revolutionary ideas and techniques. The first to have brought back a solid knowledge in this field is probably Nivedita who met Kropotkin at the turn of the 20th century and who found his views and speeches pertinent.[55] Anarchism was, in fact, the first movement to inspire the Indian revolutionaries who drew from this repertoire their own version of 'propaganda by action' and their cult of individual action. But this influence must not be exaggerated. First, the Hindu revolutionaries translated the anarchist idiom into their own grammar. This vernacularization process is evident from the interpretation of the Gita, of the ethos of the warrior-sannyasin, of the ideal of sacrifice which is spelled out in religious terms. In fact, Hindu secret societies have systematically looked for autochthonous equivalents to the western notions they were drawing their inspiration from in order to appropriate these imports more effectively. But in this process, the original concepts got diluted or transformed. This is the classic implication of the quest for equivalents mentioned above. The Indian revolutionaries fought less against the State itself – like the European anarchists – than against the *colonial* State. They soon grew tired of the ideological debates which took place in Europe anyway. Peter Heehs points out that after a month, Hem Chandra Das stopped taking part in the meetings of the anarchists that he attended in Paris in 1907 and that, when he came back to Bengal, the leaders of the movement – led by Barindra Ghosh – were much more interested in the manual that would enable them to make bombs, rather than

[55] *Ibid.*, p. 72.

in the ideas and organizational models[56] that he somewhat tried to report.[57]

5) This reinterpretation and dilution of the European revolutionary movements and ideologies – except at an emotional or even romantic level are perfectly congruent with our first conclusion, to which we have to finally return. The first Indian revolutionaries, marked by their own religious beliefs and by the fact that most of them 'only' want to get rid of the British physically. They do not mind dying in the process – on the contrary: they want to sacrifice themselves and thereby become role models. As one of those who killed Curzon-Wyllie said during his trial: 'The only thing that one must learn in today's is how to die, and the best way to teach it, is to die oneself'.[58] Many anarchists and nihilists had the same approach and till the first decade of the 20th century, they tended to prevail among the "revolutionaries".

[56] The Bengalis, nevertheless, could have improved the structure of their movements which will continue to suffer on account of endemic factionalism. The Anushilan Samiti was thus split into two in 1906 after differences cropped up between Barindra Ghosh and Pulin Das, the head of the branch in Dacca. The former started a movement named after his journal, Jugantar, while the latter retained the original name. Opposition between these two factions was not only because of their personal rivalry. It also came from a fundamental difference. While B. Ghosh gave more importance to violent action, P. Mitra remained faithful to the idea of both physical and ideological training prior to a violent action. Forced by Pulin Das, the Anushilan Samiti, however, plunged into terrorist operations which, though belated, were better conceived so that it at once succeeded in injuring very severely a British man, a Collector. What is more, a number of important 'collaborators', all of them Indians, were assassinated. The success of the Anushilan Samiti seems to be related to the centralization of the decision-making process which made the organization more efficient and less prone to indiscretions. These, sign of being too lax, will spell doom for the Jugantar group (also called the group of Maniktala), a splinter group, and more prone to plundering and even criminalizing terrorist action.

[57] *Ibid.*, p. 79 and 81.

[58] Cited in Wilfrid Seawen Blunt, *My Diaries. Being a personal narrative of events, 1888–1914*, London, 1914, Appendix II, p. 288.

However, things will change during and after WWI and even more after the 1917 Bolshevik Revolution. However, the ambiguous relation with violence noticed above and the cult of individual action (and martyrdom) at the expense of a more political (and organized) gameplan, will somewhat remain.

REPUBLICANS AND SOCIALISTS: THE COMING TO AGE OF INDIAN REVOLUTIONARIES (1914–31)

The early years of the 1910s were marked by a decline of the revolutionary movement in India. The repression had thrown a number of militants in prison and led some others to flee – to Pondicherry in the case of Aurobindo Ghosh, to Japan in the case of Rashbehari Bose.[59] Furthermore, the criminalization of the secret societies gathered pace in Bengal.[60] Quite a number of mighty notables patronized terrorist groups in exchange of assassinations whose targets were rivals and other heirs of family vendettas. The revival really came from abroad where a number of militants were in self-exile and from where they brought back a new vision of Revolution.

Reshaped by the Exiled

The Indian revolutionaries already had a base abroad thanks to the India House in London. But, following the arrest of Savarkar and other boarders, its proprietor, S.K. Varma, decided to keep the place away from this kind of activities. The most determined of the revolutionaries fell back on continental Europe. One of them, Lala Hardayal, originally from Delhi, became the leading light of first, the Geneva, and then, the Paris edition of the periodical,

[59] In 1915, R.B. Bose, one of the leaders of the Anushilan Samiti, had organized an uprising of the Indian soldiers in the army under the British command. His failure led to the arrests – in what is known as the first Lahore Conspiracy Case – of more than 50 followers (of whom 28 were hanged), while he managed to escape.

[60] Peter Heehs, op.cit., p. 29 and Leonard Gordon, 'Portrait of a Bengali revolutionary', *Journal of Asian Studies*, 1968, vol. 27, no. 2, p. 205.

Vande Mataram, where he wrote as early as 1909 that 'the centre of gravity of political activity' (for the Indian revolutionaries) had passed from Calcutta, Poona and Lahore to Paris, Geneva, Berlin, London and New York.[61] In Paris, Hardayal met Longuet, Marx's son-in-law, who worked with *L'Humanité* and who initiated him into Marxism.[62] In 1910, Hardayal travelled across the Atlantic and settled down as a professor in Stanford where he continued to take interest in the author of *Capital* and got in touch with the Indian immigrants who kept alive the revolutionary flame with the support of equally anti-English Irish activists. One of these Indians, Tarak Nath Das, brought out a newspaper *The Free Hindustan* in which he argued in favour of giving up terrorism for setting up a revolutionary organization. In 1909 he thus wrote, 'India will never gain independence simply by political assassinations'[63] – a formula that Kropotkin would not have disapproved of towards the end of his life. Hardayal, too, was aware of it. In 1912 he wrote a biography of Marx, entitled *Karl Marx: A Modern Rishi*, to be published in the prestigious *Modern Review* of Calcutta. The title is surprising, as the word 'Rishi' denotes in India *seers* (sages) of the ancient times who gave the country its first religion. But he adds in the very first page of his study that the biography intended to show how 'saintliness does not consist in simply repeating religious formulae...'[64] In fact, Hardayal was the first Indian to initiate the revolutionary movement into socialism. He is also the first to equip it with an organization supposed to be secular,

[61] Cited by Puran Chandra Joshi, "Lala Hardayal. A biographical note", in P.C. Joshi and K. Damodaran (eds.), *Marx Comes to India*, Delhi, Manohar, 1975, p. 25.

[62] Emily C. Brown, *Har Dayal: Hindu Revolutionary and Rationalist*, Tucson, The University of Arizona Press, 1975.

[63] Cited in ibid., p. 27.

[64] Lala Hardayal, 'Karl Marx: A Modern Rishi', *Modern Review*, reproduced in Puran Chandra Joshi and K. Damodaran (eds.), *Marx Comes to India*, Delhi, Manohar, 1975, p. 47.

even republican – the Ghadr Party. The pioneering character of the latter was also linked to its conception – unheard of in India – of a long-drawn guerrilla war which was in contrast with the practice of assassination attempts, prevalent till then. This Party found in World War I the opportunity to dislodge the British from India. Hardayal returned to Europe to make contacts with the Germans. But none of the plans, made jointly with the Germans or separately (delivering arms to the Bengali revolutionaries, making its way through Afghanistan, etc.) will be realized, and Hardayal gave up the idea very soon.

But by 1917, there were other potential allies for the Indian revolutionaries. M.N. Roy, a member of the Anushilan Samiti, who had left for Java to retrieve – in vain – German arms, became acquainted with American socialists in New York. Subsequently, he had to go into exile to Mexico, as the American authorities, at the insistence of the British, were in search for Indian accomplices of the Germans. In Mexico, Roy got associated with socialist networks through which he met Borodin, one of the leaders of the Bolshevik Party who was collecting financial support for the ongoing revolution. The two men were to remain friends for many years. Roy joined Borodin in Russia in 1920 to become the first Indian to participate in the Second Congress of the Comintern. This saga is just an example – certainly the most characteristic one – of the increasingly cosmopolitan dimension of the Indian revolutionary movement. M.N. Roy and others were, from now on, going to sustain Indian revolutionary organizations by providing ideological inputs and advice on organizational matters which, in turn, were going to lead to the partial transformation of the successors of the old secret societies.

Challenged by Gandhi

Besides foreign (and in particular communist) influences, another major factor of transformation of the Indian revolutionary movement which appeared in the 1920s was the emergence of

Gandhi – who assumed charge of the Congress Party in 1920 – on the political scene. An apostle of non-violence, the Mahatma, had a meeting with revolutionaries in September 1920 to ask them to let him experiment for a year with his technique and abstain from utilizing theirs. The Non-Cooperation movement will continue, in reality, till February, 1922. It mobilized various sections of society, urban as well as rural, something the revolutionaries had failed to achieve. Their modus operandi was called into question and many of them decided to take part in the Non-Cooperation Movement. One of them, Bimal Prasad Jain, declared many years later that he started to work 'with the Congress, because the independence movement had gone down to the masses and that was the only purpose of the terrorist movement – to rouse masses for a mass movement. Gandhiji played a very important role in making it a mass movement'.[65]

Besides the external impact of the communist method, based on a well-organized party having its finger on the pulse of the working class, the internal impact of the first Gandhian movement that brought thousands of supporters out in the streets, led the revolutionaries to think of a different approach.

But Gandhi showed them the way as much as it blocked it, since the Mahatma reaffirmed repeatedly the need for non-violence. For Gandhi, non-violence was a categorical imperative that he had inherited from his extensive reading of books on Christianity – from the *Sermon on the Mount* to Tolstoy – but that he also drew just as much, if not more, from the Hindu and Jain value systems, where the notion of *Ahimsa* (literally, non-violence) is cardinal. This philosophy made an impression on Gandhi at a very young age in his native Gujarat where Jainism is more widely held than elsewhere in India (except Rajasthan perhaps). The interplay of these influences did not explain exclusively the political repertoire

[65] Cited in Kama Maclean, *A Revolutionary History of Interwar India*, London, Hurst, 2015, p. 231.

of non-violence of Gandhi. If he took recourse to it, it is that the Mahatma, in a pragmatic manner, considered that no other way would help the Indians to drive the British out of the country. Indian society was too disunited and the balance of forces too unfavorable for any other alternative to succeed. This realization is found in a book, *Hind Swaraj*, that Gandhi wrote in 1908 to dissuade the Indian youth from embracing the revolutionary cause at a time when terrorist attacks were on the rise. In this book, he considers that 'brutal force is not natural on Indian soil'[66] and that, in any case given the conditions created by the Raj, 'strength of mind is superior to that of arms'.[67] He finds it preferable to set himself up as the moral victim of violence – both symbolic and physical – of the colonial ruler in order to mobilize the masses and to put the blame on the foreign oppressor so much so that the latter ends up by feeling guilty and by giving in. It was through sacrifice that Gandhi wanted to restore the dignity of his nation – and even to create it to some extent –, as well as to free it psychologically, and then politically, from the colonial ruler.[68]

If the 'Extremists' found one justification for their defence of violence in the Gita, Gandhi drew his inspiration from the same book which, for him, 'has demonstrated the futility of violence'.[69] In the Introduction to his translation of the Gita in Gujarati, he underlines that:

> Let it be granted that according to the letter of the Gita it is possible that warfare is consistent with the renunciation of fruit [of

[66] Mohandas Karamchand Gandhi, *Indian Home Rule*, Madras, Ganesh, 1922, p. 110.

[67] Ibid., p. 90.

[68] Lloyd I. Rudolph and Susanne H. Rudolph, *The Modernity of Tradition: Political Development in India*, Chicago, The University of Chicago Press, 1967, p. 161; Ashis Nandy, *At the Edge of Psychology. Essays in Politics and Culture*, Delhi-Oxford, Oxford University Press, 1980, pp. 73–75.

[69] B.R. Nanda, *Gandhi and Religion*, New Delhi, Oxford University Press, 1990, p. 5.

> action]. But after 40 years' unremitting endeavour fully to enforce the teaching of the Gita in my own life, I have in all humility felt that perfect renunciation is impossible without perfect observance of *ahimsa* in every shape and form.[70]

Tilak, who was a witness to the rise in power of Gandhi before his death in 1920, strongly opposed the Mahatma, especially after the latter introduced him in his journal, *Young India*, as someone for whom the end justified the means – a judgment to which the concerned retorted sharply:

> Politics is a game of worldly people and not of sadhus and instead of the maxim, Akkodhena jine kodham (conquer anger by non-anger) as preached by Buddha, I prefer to rely on the maxim of Shri Krishna, Ye yatha maam prapadyante taannstathaira bhajamyahang (I give to them reward in the same manner and to the same extent that they worship me).[71]

Two political cultures thus clashed in 1920. That of Tilak justified recourse to violence against the British on the basis of a sharp sense of *realpolitik* and at the same time imbued with religious references. That of Gandhi extoled ahimsa in accordance with other religious references. The revolutionary movement continued to be inspired by the former but was somewhat delegitimized by the latter. Some adjustment had to take place for this reason and because of the socialist influences mentioned above.

The Hindustan Republican Association: Between Ancients and Moderns

In February 1922, Gandhi suspended the Non-Cooperation Movement as a reaction to militants setting fire to a police post at Chauri Chaura (United Provinces). For Gandhi, Chauri

[70] Cited by Mysore Narasimhachar Srinivas, 'Gandhi's religion', *Economic and Political Weekly*, June 24, 1995, p. 1490.

[71] Cited by Narayan Gopal Jog, *Lokamanya Bal Gangadhar Tilak*, New Delhi, Ministry of Information & Broadcasting, 1979, p. 199.

Chaura signified a criminal blunder even justifying repentance on his part. The Mahatma's attitude made the revolutionaries feel indignant. Some of them decided to re-launch their movement and to capitalize on the fact that many supporters of the Non-Cooperation Movement had been deceived by the retreat of the Mahatma.[72] They based their new organizations on ideas coming from the West, but did not break with the legacy of the secret societies, including the Anushilan Samiti.

In fact, Bengalis from this organization who had settled down in the United Provinces and Punjab played an important role in the making of the Hindustan Republican Association,[73] which was founded in 1924 and shifted the epicentre of the revolutionary movement to the United Provinces (where the Anushilan Samiti had already opened branches) and to the Punjab (where the Arya Samaj had prepared the ground for such a development). Ideologically, the references of the HRA were republicanism and socialism, the Russian Revolution exerting upon them an increasing influence, even if the American and the French ones enjoyed the benefits of being the predecessors. But the HRA remained true to some values of the old anarcho-terrorist techniques of the Hindu secret societies.

In 1924, the revolutionaries of the United Provinces and Punjab who formed the HR specified in the movement's constitution that their aim was 'to establish a federal republic of the United States of India by an organized and armed revolution'.[74] The

[72] Chandrasekhar Azad, who had joined the Freedom Movement attracted by Gandhi – whose name he yelled with each lash from the police for having participated in the non-cooperation movement at the age of 15 – distanced himself from the Congress and became a revolutionary after the Mahatma suspended the non-cooperation movement. (See I. Mallikarjuna Sharma, *op.cit.*, p. 185)

[73] David Laushey, *Bengal Terrorism and the Marxist Left. Aspects of Regional Nationalism in India, 1905–1942*, Calcutta, Firma K. L. Mukhopadhyaya, 1975, p. 34.

[74] Cited by S. Irfan Habib, *To make the deaf hear. Ideology and programme of Bhagat Singh and his comrades, Gurgaon, Three Essays*, 2007, p. 22.

two architects of the movement – both of Bengali origin – Jogesh Chandra Chatterjee and S.N. Sanyal, were in contact with M.N. Roy[75]. While the former was acquainted with the writings of Werner Sombart, the latter had read Bukharin extensively.[76] The ideological charter of the movement was published on 1st January 1925 as *The Manifesto of the Hindustan Republican Association* also known as *The Revolutionary.* This programme of action was inspired not only by socialism but also by the most radical internationalism:

> The revolutionary party is not national but international in the sense that its ultimate object is to bring harmony in the world by respecting and guaranteeing the diverse interests of the different nations. It aims not at competition but at co-operation between the different nations and states ....[77]

Besides this new approach, the Indian revolutionaries still remained under the influence of the cult of violence and a form of anarchism. According to them, only chaos could wipe the slate clean in order to make a fresh start. *The Manifesto of the Hindustan Republican Association,* therefore, opened with these words of Nietzsche, 'Chaos is necessary to the birth of a new star '. It then goes on to analyse this formula in its own way: 'India is also taking a new birth, and is passing through that inevitable phase, when chaos, and agony shall play their destined role, when all calculations shall prove futile, when the wise and mighty shall be bewildered by the simple and the weak, when great empires shall crumble down, and new nations shall arise and surprise humanity with the splendour and glory which shall be all its own'.[78]

A deeper contradiction existed between the internationalism flaunted by the HRA and its deep-rooted and passionate nationalism.

[75] I. Mallikarjuna Sharma, op.cit., p. 187.
[76] Cited by S. Irfan Habib, op.cit., p. 22.
[77] Cited by S. Irfan Habib, op.cit., p. 193.
[78] Cited by S. Irfan Habib, op.cit., p. 191.

This tension was partially resolved by its fundamental objective: to build in India a new man for the betterment of the entire world. But the new man in question remained very Indian! Certainly, the society of the future had to be a socialist one and the exploitation of man by man be abolished by the nationalization of the means of production. But socialist culture was not supposed to do away with all the past traditions, particularly those inspired by religion. The HRA did not seek to secularize society. What the leaders of the HRA condemned was not religion but 'communalism', in particular when it manifested itself in an aggressive proselytism.

Respect for religion found expression in some explicit references to Hinduism. For instance, Sanyal wrote in *The Manifesto of the Hindustan Republican Association:* '[The revolutionary party] follows the footsteps of great Indian Rishis of the glorious past and of Bolshevik Russia in the modern age'.[79] Sanyal was greatly impressed by the political economy of Karl Marx, but did not accept materialism. In fact, his internationalism was itself a variant of Hindu universalism, this religion being perceived as delivering a message to the entire world. Irfan Habib very pertinently points out that 'Sanyal believed India had been waiting for a Krishna [one of the avatars of Vishnu] who could offer a new ideal that would be followed not only by India by India but by the humanity as a whole ...'.[80]

If the leaders of the HRA did not distance themselves from the religious culture of their society – and even make it the philosophical base of their revolutionary ideal –, they did break away from the ritualism of the Anushilan Samiti or the other secret societies which was practiced since the beginning of the 20th century. A similar reorientation was observed in connection with their long-term programmes. In spite of their fascination

[79] Cited by S. Irfan Habib, op.cit., p. 193.

[80] Cited by S. Irfan Habib, op.cit., p. 27. This assessment is based on a letter that Sanyal had written to Gandhi and which was published in Gandhi's journal *Young India* on 12 February 1925.

for chaos, the HRA emphasized organizational work so as to transform itself into a mass movement. *The Manifesto of the Hindustan Republican Association* pointed out that 'The Indian revolutionaries are neither terrorists nor anarchists (...) They do not believe that terrorism alone can bring independence and they do not want terrorism for terrorism's sake although they may at time resort to this method as a very effective means of retaliation'[81]. The HRA, therefore, initiated a transition. It maintained a new kind of rapport with violence and religion. The Hindustan Socialist Republican Association (HRSA) that was to emerge from it will complete the transition to some extent.

The HRSA, Socialism and Violence

In the mid-1920s, the Kakori Conspiracy Case[82] left the movement headless, as all its front-ranking leaders, including Sanyal, were arrested and sent to the gallows or to jail. The following generation of militants who were to revive the movement was of a different kind. The strongest personality in this group, Bhagat Singh, bears witness to it. Born in Lyallpur (Punjab) to a Sikh family that came under the influence of the Arya Samaj and the Ghadr Party – his uncle, Ajit Singh had been deported to Mandalay along with Lajpat Rai when he was a child. Bhagat Singh had his training at the National College of Lahore.[83] He was particularly shocked by the Jallianwallah Bagh massacre at Amritsar in 1919, where General Dyer killed hundreds of people. He then took part in the

[81] Cited by S. Irfan Habib, op.cit., p. 195.

[82] This case in named after a small town of today's Uttar Pradesh where, in 1925, HRA operatives stopped a train to rob the government's money it was transporting. The accidental murder of one of the passengers made it a criminal case. About 40 HRA members were arrested, four of them were sentenced to death, two of them, including S.N. Sanyal were sent to the Port Blair cellular jail in the Andaman and another dozen were condemned to up to 14 years of imprisonment.

[83] Gopal Thakur, *Bhagat Singh. The Man and His Ideas*, New Delhi, People's Publishing House, 1976.

Non-Cooperation Movement[84] and – like many others – joined the revolutionary movement after its suspension by Mahatma Gandhi. In 1926, he started the Naujawan Bharat Sabha as an affiliate of the HSRA and tried to draw in its fold the youth of the province in order to develop a socialist and non-religious organization. In its first manifesto, his socialism, still very rudimentary, appears as a humanist response:

> ... India, with land and the richest mineral resources, is today one of the poorest countries. India, that could have felt proud of being one of the most glorious civilizations, is today the most backward countries, its literacy rate being just 5%. Does it require any authorities to prove that India, with the richest soil land mines, is today one of the poorest, that India which could be proud of so glorious a civilisation is today the most backward country with only 5% literacy? Do not the people know that India has to pay the largest toll of human life with the highest child death rate in the world? The epidemics like plague, cholera, influenza and such other diseases are becoming common day by day.[85]

If the British were naturally the special target of Bhagat Singh, he also puts the blame on his compatriots, paralysed with superstitions:

> A branch of peepal tree is cut and religious feelings of the Hindus are injured. A corner of a paper idol, tazia, of the idol-breaker Mohammedans is broken, and 'Allah' gets enraged, who cannot be satisfied with anything less than the blood of the infidel Hindus. Man should receive more attention than the beasts and yet, in India, people break their heads in the name of sacred beasts.[86]

The combination of socialism, humanism and nationalism that was the trade mark of Bhagat Singh, was going to become strong

[84] Which resulted in his leaving the DAV College to join the National College started by Lajpat Rai.

[85] "Manifesto of the Naujawan Bharat Sabha, Punjab", Annexure C-2 od S. Irfan Habib, op.cit., p. 198.

[86] See S. Irfan Habib, op.cit., pp. 199–200.

after the revival, in September, 1928, of the HRA under another name, the Hindustan Socialist Republican Association (HRSA). While Bhagat Singh remained the key figure of the HSRA, among its leaders were other outstanding men, including Sukhdev, a great admirer of communism, Vijay Kumar Sinha – an avid reader, Shiv Verma and Chandrashekhar Azad, a former HRA leader who was in charge of the Association's 'military' operations. These men formed a Central Committee in which seated two representatives of the provinces where the movement was well established, Punjab, United Provinces and Bihar. The organization was at once divided into two branches – ideological and military. Bhagat Singh was at the helm of the former but took part in the latter too. Indeed, he was directly involved in the assassination of J.P. Saunders, a policeman who had been mistaken for the police chief, J. A. Scott, whom Bhagat Singh held responsible for the death of Lala Lajpat Rai. An Arya Samajist and a Congress leader, Lajpat Rai had been killed after a *lathi* charge while he demonstrated against the visit of the Simon Commission in Lahore. Like the terrorist of the 19th century, the HRSA considered – in an 'official' communiqué – that, by killing Saunders, it could 'let the world know that India still lives; that the blood of youths has not been totally cooled down and that they can still risk their lives if the honour of their nation is at stake'[87]. This is well in tune with the quest for self-esteem and the 'propaganda by action' that was associated with Anushilan Samiti and other terrorist groups.

But Bhagat Singh made the transition from terrorism to revolution. In his last piece of writing – drafted in February 1931 – he refers to his past action in a very telling manner:

> Apparently I have acted as a terrorist. But I am not a terrorist. I am a revolutionary who has got such definite ideas of a lengthy programme (...) Let me announce with all the strength at my

[87] Chandra Shekhar Azad, 'Hindustan Socialist Republican Association Notice', in Bhagat Singh, op. cit., p. 20.

> command, that I am not a terrorist and never was, [except] perhaps in the beginning of my revolutionary career.[88]

Bhagat Singh's worldview had been reshaped in the meantime by readings of a rare variety. The list of authors in his library shows many books by various Western authors. One finds there Marx, Engels, Trotsky, Alfred Barton, Thomas Paine, Upton Sinclair, Morris Hillquit, Jack London, Theodor Hertzka, Patrick McGill, Scott Nearing, Victor Hugo, Dostoevsky, Bipin Chandra Pal, Valentine Chirol, Spinoza, Henry van Dyke, Bertrand Russell, John Stuart Mill, Thomas Jefferson, Kautsky, Bukharin, Burke, Lenin, Thomas d'Aquinas, Locke, Austin, Danton, Charles Edwards Russell, Omar Khayyam, James Russell Lowell, William Wordsworth, Lord Tennyson, V.N. Figner, Tagore, N.A. Morozov, Horace Greeley, Wendell Phillips, Frederic Harrison, J. Campbell, George D. Herron, Herbert Spencer, Henry Maine and Rousseau.[89]

These books that Bhagat Singh read in jail contributed to make him a rationalist and a socialist. He was the first revolutionary to express clearly his rejection of religion in a magnificent text, 'Why I am an atheist', written in prison – just when he was condemned to death (see below) – in response to a fellow prisoner who offered to pray for him (something quite useless in the eyes of Bhagat Singh).[90] In this very personal text, Bhagat Singh pays homage to his comrades who believe in God, starting with Sanyal, whose 'mysticism' he remembers, then Pandit Ram Prasad Bismil (a key player of the Kakori conspiracy case who was sentenced to death), whose religious beliefs originated in his 'orthodox Arya

[88] Bhagat Singh, 'To young political workers', in Bhagat Singh, op. cit., pp. 101–02.

[89] This list remains incomplete: readings that reveal the notes taken, while in prison, by this young man, executed at the age of 24, are literally encyclopedic (See "The Jail Notebook" *in Shiv* Verma [ed.], *Bhagat Singh. On the Path to Liberation*, Chennai, Bhrati Puthakalayam, 2007, pp. 221–329.)

[90] This text, published in *The People* of 27 September 1931, is reproduced as Annexure B-3 of S. Irfan Habib, op.cit. pp. 155–78.

Samaj' or Rajendra Nath Lahiri (another architect of the Kakori conspiracy case who was also executed), and who 'could not suppress his desire of reciting hymns of the Upanishads and the Gita'.[91] Bhagat Singh considers that he himself was 'a romantic and an idealist revolutionary' till 1926. His 'turning' to another direction, he feels, came with the reading of some of the above-mentioned authors.[92]

The rationalist Bhagat Singh cites Darwin when it comes to explaining the origin of man from the time of the evolution of the species.[93] He states lucidly how he awaits death without hoping for a life beyond:

> A God-believing Hindu might be expecting to be reborn as a king, a Muslim or a Christian, might dream of the luxuries to be enjoyed in paradise and the reward he is to get for his sufferings and sacrifices. But what am I to expect? I know the moment the rope is fitted round my neck and rafters removed, from under my feet. That will be the final moment – that will be the last moment. I, or to be more precise, my soul, as interpreted in the metaphysical terminology, shall all be finished there. Nothing further. A short life of struggle with no such magnificent end, shall in itself be the reward if I have the courage to take it in that light. That is all. With no selfish motive, or desire to be awarded here or hereafter, quite disinterestedly have I devoted my life to the cause of independence, because I could not do otherwise. The day we find a great number of men and women with this psychology who cannot devote themselves to anything else than the service of mankind and emancipation of the suffering humanity; that day shall inaugurate the era of liberty.[94]

The non-belief in the beyond and agnosticism in the name of cold rationalism make Bhagat Singh accept his death sentence as

[91] Ibid., p. 158.
[92] Ibid., p. 159.
[93] Ibid. p. 168.
[94] Reproduced *in* S. Irfan Habib, op.cit., p. 161.

if it was that of someone else and this distancing of oneself with a striking lucidity reflects better than anything else the birth of a revolutionary of a new genre. In fact, Bhagat Singh, with great candour, presents himself as an example, his sacrifice serving, above all, as a model to emulate.

Bhagat Singh's rejection of religion in the (Marxist) sense in which he sees it, as a creed that alienates the masses, goes together with his socialist criticism of society as much as with his criticism of Hinduism, not only from a metaphysical but also from a social viewpoint.[95] Here, he breaks away from his predecessors by, at the same time, strongly criticizing two systems of oppression – capitalism and caste – while till then the Indian revolutionaries had only targeted capitalism and colonialism.[96]

In 1930, in a statement sent to the judges who had just convicted him and B.K. Dutt in the Assembly Bomb Case (see below), he gives his definition of 'Revolution' for the first time:

> Bombs and pistols do not make (a) Revolution. That is not our understanding. The sword of Revolution is sharpened on the whetting-stone of ideas, and this is what we wished to emphasise. Revolution is the means to end the miseries brought on by capitalist wars'.[97] In February 1931, Bhagat Singh went further, inviting the Indian youth, in a specially drafted manifesto, to embrace Marxism. Referring to the statement mentioned above, Bhagat Singh repeats that, 'Revolution means the complete overthrow of the existing social order and its replacement with the socialist order. For that purpose our immediate aim is the achievement of power. As a matter of fact, the state, the government machinery is

[95] *Ibid.*, pp. 166–67.

[96] Bhagat Singh had started his fight against the caste system since the establishment of the Naujawan Bharat Sabha which, for example, used to organize feasts attended by people of different castes and different religions – and also served occasionally both the halal and the jhalka meat (S. Irfan Habib, op.cit., p. 43.)

[97] Bhagat Singh, 'Statement before the Lahore High Court bench', in Bhagat Singh op. cit., p. 65.

> just a weapon in the hands of the ruling class to further safeguard its interest. We want to snatch and handle it to utilize it for the consummation of our ideal, i.e., social reconstruction on new, i.e. Marxist basis.[98]

In fact, Bhagat Singh is a Janus-like figure combining different sources of inspiration, some of them Marxist, others harking back to the "propaganda by action". This is evident from his last deed – and the fact that he subsequently assumed it as a relevant action till his death. On 8 April 1929, he, along with B.K. Dutt threw two bombs in the Central Legislative Assembly, 'to make the deaf hear', as written on the tracts they distributed in the Assembly after their lightening coup.[99] This formula was borrowed from Auguste Vaillant, a French anarchist. But Bhagat Singh also presented this action as being part of a larger game plan. First, it was aimed at dissuading the Assembly from voting for a law, namely, The Public Safety and Trade Disputes Bill, whose implementation would have penalized Indian workers. Second, it was also aimed, by and large, to denounce the manner in which this so-called Indian Parliament projected itself to be an accomplice of the British. Finally, it aimed at avenging the death of Lajpat Rai. All these explanations relate this act as much to the anarchist as to the socialist agenda. The former dimension is obvious in the fact that he wanted, thanks to this 'propaganda by action' to project himself as a martyr and the hero of a cause that would thus win over new supporters. This stands out clearly from the letter in which Bhagat Singh, from his cell, strongly reproached his father for trying to obtain clemency from the British. He refused mercy, refused life – till the very end. He wished that his trial should remain in the annals of history as a moment when contempt of law clearly appeared as the act of the British and he wished nothing else but to die like a martyr

[98] Bhagat Singh, "To young political workers", in ibid., pp. 88-9.
[99] 'To make the deaf hear', Annexure B-1 of S. Irfan Habib, op.cit. p. 145.

of this inhuman rule. To clearly set himself apart from what he considered to be only giving in to weakness on the part of his father, he asked him to publish his letter.[100] Bhagat Singh, indeed, became a hero and a rallying point for the entire Indian nation. His co-accused, Ajoy Ghosh, while coming out of prison (for he had been acquitted) discovered that, 'His name was on the lips of the millions, his image in the heart of all the young men'.[101] A large number of Indians joined Bhagat Singh's struggle, inspired by his example[102]. In that sense, Bhagat Singh operated like the 19th century terrorists.

The other side of the coin, however, shows that Bhagat Singh did not valorise violence. To have a proper understanding of his political philosophy one must read till the end the leaflet that Bhagat Singh and Dutt threw in the Assembly after hurling their bombs. Its concluding words are remarkable:

> We are sorry to admit that we who attach so great a sanctity to human life, who dream of a glorious future, when man will be enjoying perfect peace and full liberty, have been forced to shed human blood.[103]

These words reveal a denial of violence that would take a more systematic form in the declaration of Singh and Dutt before the Judges. There, they would emphasize that the two bombs had been thrown at the unoccupied rows and that their composition – the details of which they provide, like great chemists – made them inoffensive: 'had they been loaded with some other high explosive, with a charge of destructive pellets or darts, they

[101] Bhagat Singh, 'Letter to father', in Shiv Verma (ed.), op.cit., pp. 169–71.

[101] Ajay Ghosh, "A fraud of an ordinance", in ibid., p. 174.

[102] The veteran of the communist movement, Har Kishan Singh Surjeet, thus remembers in 1995 how, after the execution of Bhagat Singh, he at once discontinued his studies to join the revolutionary movement ('Foreword', *in* Shiv Verma (ed.), op.cit., p. 10.)

[103] S. Irfan Habib, op.cit., p. 146.

would have sufficed to wipe out a majority of the Members of the Legislative Assembly'.[104]

Singh and Dutt even defend themselves against their recourse to violence – they merely speak of 'force':

> We are next to none in our love for humanity. Far from having any malice against any individual, we hold human life sacred beyond words (...) Our sole purpose was 'to make the deaf hear' and to give the heedless a timely warning (...) We have only marked the end of an era of Utopian non-violence, of whose futility the rising generation has been convinced beyond the shadow of doubt (...) Force when aggressively applied is 'violence' and is therefore, morally unjustifiable, but when it is used in the furtherance of a legitimate cause, it has its moral justification (...) Despite the evidence of the government expert, the bombs that were thrown in the Assembly Chamber resulted in slight damage to an empty bench and some slight abrasions in less than half a dozen cases. While government scientists and experts have ascribed this result to a miracle, we see nothing but a precisely scientific process in this incident. Firstly, the two bombs exploded in vacant spaces within the wooden barriers of the desks and benches; secondly, even those who were within two feet of the explosion, for instance, Mr. P. Rau, Mr. Shankar Rao and Sir George Schuster, were either not hurt or only slightly scratched (...) We then deliberately offered ourselves to bear the penalty for what we had done and let the imperialist exploiters know that by crushing individuals, they cannot kill ideas. By crushing two insignificant units, a nation cannot be crushed. (...) 'Revolution' does not necessarily involve sanguinary strife, nor is there any place in it for individual vendetta. It is not the cult of the bomb and the pistol. By 'Revolution' we mean that the present order of things, which is based on manifest injustice, must change (...) The whole edifice of this civilization, if not saved in time, shall crumble. A radical change, therefore, is necessary and

[104] 'Statement in the sessions court', op.cit., pp. 151–52.

> it is the duty of those who realize it to reorganize society on the socialistic basis. Unless this thing is done and the exploitation of man by man and of nations by nations is brought to an end, sufferings and carnage with which humanity is threatened today cannot be prevented (...) At the altar of this Revolution we have brought our youth as an incense, for no sacrifice is too great for so magnificent a cause. We are content, we await the advent of Revolution.
>
> Long Live the Revolution!"[105]

This text is paradigmatic. It reconfirms the shift of the Indian revolutionaries from terrorism to socialism, but it qualifies their view of violence in a new manner. Not only is violence not useful (in the sense that it cannot bring about social change), but it is despicable in moral terms because life is sacred. This approach is well in tune with Hindu ideals and not very different from Gandhi's perspective. Like the Mahatma, Bhagat Singh emphasizes the value of his *sacrifice* – instead of the killing of his enemies. And like the Mahatma, he refers to Christian values and the figure of Jesus Christ who sacrificed himself for saving the humanity. In his statement before the Lahore High Court he declared: 'If we set aside motive, then Jesus Christ will appear a man responsible for breaking peace and preaching revolt, and a dangerous personality in the language of the law. But we worship him. He commands great respect and a place in our hearts; the sight of his image fills us with spiritual energy'.[106] This revolutionary invocation of Jesus-Christ is not unique. Three weeks after Bhagat Singh, Rajguru and Sukhdev were executed on 24 March 1931, a conference of India's martyrs was held in Paradise – according to the Lahore-based Urdu newspaper, *Vir Bharat*. Jesus Christ attended it, as if he was one of them, that made for a very interesting scene:

[105] Ibid., pp. 148–54.

[106] 'Statement before the Lahore High Court Bench', in Bhagat Singh, op. cit., p. 59.

> Sardar Bhagat Singh said: 'India's martyr greet the martyr of Jerusalem.' Voices were raised by the Jallianwallah Bagh martyrs: 'Accept our salutation O peaceful shepherd of bloody thirsty sheep'. The Sholapur men said: 'Turn your wolves into sheep again'. In short the welkin (sic) resounded with shouts like the above. Jesus met every one cordially and after kissing the Cross he said: 'An innocent man's blood never goes in vain'. Dyer is to-day being burnt in hell fire. He is crying to me for intercession but can I intercede on the behalf of executioners, murderers and assassins? I swear by this sacred Cross that there is absolutely no nearness between me and these white people whose hearts have become black with the blood of oppressed people. They will get their desserts and no heavenly power can save them from the wrath of my Holy Father. Rest assured, God will never forgive your murderers.
>
> After having made the above remarks Jesus patted Sardar Bhagat Singh and gave benedictions to all the martyrs. (...)

In the course of his speech Martyr Khudi Ram Bose, representing the martyrs of Bengal, said:

> I wish I could again take birth in the Mother Country and sacrifice my life to cut asunder the chains of Bharat Mata. The war of Mahabharat is again in progress in India. A peaceful man like Mahatma Gandhi cannot quarrel with anyone. He is simply working as the tool of this Just God. The disc of Lord Krishna is working and British rule is coming to an end in India every moment. Lord Krishna is drinking the blood of the witch of slavery and munching her bones.[107]

This oneirocritic presentation is revealing of the desire of the revolutionaries to combine violence and non-violence. They remained attached to violent methods, but they were sensitive to the value and prestige of non-violence.

[107] The full version of this "conference" is appended to Maclean, op. cit., pp. 240–41.

VIOLENCE vs NON-VIOLENCE?

While the Indian revolutionaries shifted from terrorism to socialism, they did not valorize violence like other leftists who, elsewhere in the world, had no inhibition so far as the physical elimination of remnants of the old order was concerned – see some of the French Revolutionaries after 1789 or some of the Bolsheviks after 1917. In fact, as early as the 1920s, the denial of violence came up recurrently in the discourse of the Indian revolutionaries. That was largely due to the emphasis on the merit of non-violence that Gandhi had introduced in the Indian public lexicon.

The Mahatma, for whom the end never justified the means, rose up against the series of assassination attempts that marked the end of the 1920s. In an article of *Young India* he denounced 'the cult of the bomb', following a failed attempt at assassinating Viceroy Irwin in December, 1929. Irwin came out unhurt but someone else died. The Indian revolutionaries appeared to be on the defensive, but reacted in a very telling way. B.C. Vohra gave Gandhi a reply in an article entitled "The Philosophy of the Bomb", which claimed that a common root unites Gandhian *ahimsa* and the revolutionaries' techniques:

> Violence is physical force applied for committing injustice, and this is certainly not what the revolutionaries stand for. On the other hand, what generally goes by the name of non-violence is in reality the theory of soul-force, as applied to the attainment of personal and national rights through courting suffering and hoping thus to finally convert your opponent to your point of view. When a revolutionary believes certain things to be his right he asks for them, pleads for them, argues for them, wills to attain them with all the soul-force at his command, stands the greatest amount of suffering for them, is always prepared to make the highest sacrifice for their attainment, and also backs his efforts with all the physical force he is capable of. You may coin what other word you like to describe his methods but you cannot

call it violence, because that would constitute an outrage on the dictionary meaning of that word. Satyagraha is insistence upon truth. Why press, for the acceptance of truth, by soul-force alone? Why not add physical force also to it?[108]

Such a discourse reflects the influence of the Gandhian repertoire on the revolutionaries who, however, managed to come up with an alternative discourse legitimizing their action as not violent (if not non-violent). They explained that physical force exerted against others was not the same as violence as long as it had a legitimate objective.[109]

Not only was terrorism was not seen as violent, but it was only one preliminary step towards revolution. For Vohra it is 'a phase, an inevitable and necessary phase, of the revolution'.[110] Bhagat Singh made that important point very clear in his last text called, "To the Young Political Workers". There he writes that if 'the military wing of the Party must always keep ready all the material of the war which will be at one's disposal in case of urgency [...] it must support the political activities of the Party. It cannot and should not work in an independent manner'.[111]

Clearly, Bhagat Singh is taking the revolutionaries towards a *political* understanding of their mission. And to be more political, for him, meant that their action should not be radically different from that of Gandhi's Congress. He not only somewhat, discreetly,

[108] 'The Philosophy of the Bomb', Annexure C-3 of S. Irfan Habib, op.cit., p. 206.

[109] Going further, the HSRA did not consider terrorism as an end in itself. Vohra wrote, for instance: 'Terrorism instils fear in the hearts of the oppressors, it brings hopes of revenge and redemption to the oppressed masses, it gives courage and self-confidence to the wavering, it shatters the spell of the superiority of the ruling class and raises the status of the subject race in the eyes of the world, because it is the most convincing proof of a nation's hunger for freedom'.

[110] 'The Philosophy of the Bomb', Annexure C-3, reproduced *in* S. Irfan Habib, op.cit., p. 207.

[111] 'To the Young Political Workers', Annexure B-5, reproduced *in* S. Irfan Habib, op.cit., p. 189.

admired 'the Great Gandhi'[112] for having mobilized the masses like never before, but Bhagat Singh appreciated also the work of the most progressive Congressmen, including the Nehrus.[113] He looked at them as his leaders. Explaining why he had thrown his bombs in deserted sections of the Assembly in 1929, he argued: 'Had we no idea of the strength of the bombs we were using, would we have flung them into a Chamber where respected national leaders like Pandit Motilal Nehru, Shri Kelkar, Shri Jayakar and Shri Jinnah were present? Would we have risked the lives of our leaders?'[114] After all, Bhagat Singh had decided to kill a British police chief in order to avenge a Congress leader, Lajpat Rai, to whom his uncle had been particularly close.

In fact, Bhagat Singh was less critical of the non-violent repertoire of the Congress as he was of its socio-economic conservatism. In the statement he prepared for his defence in the Lahore conspiracy case, he made it clear that the method was not the issue because revolutionaries cherished peace as much as others:

> As regards the methods, peaceful or otherwise, to be adopted for the consummation of the revolutionary ideal, let us declare that the choice rests with those who hold power. Revolutionaries, by virtue of their altruistic principles, are lovers of peace – a genuine and permanent peace based on justice and equality...[115]

Such a discourse suggests that since Bhagat Singh supported 'peaceful' means, revolutionaries and Congressmen could work together. Incidentally, when Bhagat Singh criticized the Congress for negotiating with the British in 1931 he did not ask for much more than the left wing of the party had: universal franchise

[112] Ibid., p. 182.

[113] Ibid., pp. 181–82.

[114] 'Statement before the Lahore High Court Bench', in Bhagat Singh, op. cit., p. 66.

[115] 'Statement of the undefended accused', in Bhagat Singh, op. cit., pp. 74–75.

and parliamentary democracy. He even did not rule out some compromises because, for the revolutionaries, 'compromise never means surrender, but a step forward and some rest'.[116] For Bhagat Singh, Lenin himself had shown that 'compromise is an essential weapon which has to be wielded every now and then as the struggle develops'.[117]

In fact, the difference between the Revolutionaries and Congress was more of degree than of nature. Politically, the former wanted to reach independence faster and, more importantly, socially they were for more radical changes. For Bhagat Singh, the fact that the Congressmen did not make 'any effort to organize the peasants or the labourers' showed that 'they never meant a complete revolution'.[118]Bhagat Singh plainly said: 'It is this half-heartedness that we hate'. For him, like for Dr Ambedkar at the same time, it meant that independence would make no difference in socio-political terms. It would replace one elite group by another: 'What difference [does it make to] a peasant if Sir Tej Bahadur Sapru replaces Lord Irwin?'.[119]

This is why Bhagat Singh thought that a new party had to be created. From his prison where he had only a month left before his execution, Bhagat Singh described the technique to be followed by the revolutionaries in (Bolshevik) terms – which stood in stark contrast with his anarchist legacy:

> We require – to use the term so dear to Lenin – the "professional revolutionaries", whole-time workers who have no other ambitions or life-work except the revolution [...]. The party shall have iron discipline and it need not necessarily be an underground party, rather the contrary.[120]

[116] "To Young Political Workers", in Bhagat Singh, op. cit., p. 93.

[117] Ibid. p. 84.

[118] Ibid., p. 87.

[119] Ibid., pp. 96–97.

[120] 'To the Young Political Workers', Annexure B-5, reproduced *in* S. Irfan Habib, op. cit., p. 186.

This party did not see the light of the day and Congress, therefore, remained the undeclared partner of the revolutionaries.

The Revolutionaries and the Congress: Opposing Complementarities

The revolutionaries looked at themselves more as a kind of *avant-garde* of the Congress as political rivals. Kama Maclean emphasizes that: 'Almost all HSRA members had been Congress workers in the early 1920s and had taken part in the Non-Cooperation Movement and it is widely acknowledged that Gandhi's reaction to the violence at Chauri Chaura provided the greatest fillip to revolutionary organization. However, even after the formation of the HSRA, its members continued to attend annual Congress meetings, not only to liaise with sympathisers, but also to calibrate their own activism accordingly…'.[121]

Indeed, the commonly accepted divide between a legalist Congress believing in non-violence and a revolutionary movement constraint to clandestinity and adept of terrorism is a myth. The Congress has always had in its rungs, leaders sympathizing with the underground revolutionary movement. It was evident before the coming of Gandhi on the political scene, when extremists such as Tilak and Lajpat Rai inspired and protected activists who supported violence while the latter supported the former. This remained true after Gandhi took over the control of the Congress when to his great displeasure, C.R. Das (Mayor of Calcutta), and later Subhas Chandra Bose, his successor, defended the revolutionaries. Bose, when he was the Mayor of Calcutta,[122] gave employment to a number of revolutionaries. Apart from these few famous personalities a number of Congress cadres admitted that they had supported revolutionaries, including Ganesh Shankar Vidyarthi, the Congress leader of Kanpur whose newspaper office

[121] Kama Maclean, op. cit., pp. 106–07.

[122] I. Mallikarjuna Sharma, op.cit., p. 179.

was a rendezvous for revolutionaries, like Bhagat Singh and Azad in the mid-1920s.[123]

In 1924, when Gopinath Saha was executed for having assassinated a European (who he mistook for a Police Commissioner notorious for his cruelty), the Bengali branch of Congress passed a resolution whose convoluted turn of phrase is explained by the moral judgment of Gandhi, but whose political meaning remained powerful:

> This Assembly, while denouncing and disassociating itself from violence, and, therefore, in adhering to the principle of non-violence, appreciates the ideal of self-sacrifice of Gopinath even if it goes against the larger interests of the country.[124]

The authority of Gandhi was even more directly affected when he puts to vote a resolution condemning the assassination attempt on Irwin during the plenary session of the Congress in December, 1929: it won only by a majority of 81 votes out of 1,713 voters. For Vohra, 'this demonstrated, without a shade of doubt, how solidly the country supports the revolutionaries'.[125]

Even fervent Gandhians like the Nehrus helped the revolutionaries.[126] Azad, for instance, got money from Jawaharlal in 1931 in order to send some of his comrades to Russia and get the right training.[127] When Azad was killed one week later, Purushottamdas Tandon, the President of the UP Congress Committee, 'collected Azad's ashes and organized a procession through Allahabad, culminating in a public meeting in Purushottamdas Park, where

[123] M.L. Bhargava, *Ganesh Shankar Vidyarthi*, New Delhi, Government of India, 1988, p. 44.

[124] Cited by I. Mallikarjuna Sharma, op.cit., p. 175.

[125] 'To the Young Political Workers', Annexure B-5, reproduced *in* S. Irfan Habib, op.cit., p. 189 and 209.

[126] On the popularity of Motilal among Indian revolutionaries, see Kama Maclean, op. cit., p. 150.

[127] Ibid., p. 176.

Kamla Nehru and Mrs Sachindranath Sanyal, "the wife of a notorious terrorist convict" [Sachindra Nath], addressed a meeting organized by the Allahabad Students Association"'.[128]

Not only was the Congress quite sympathetically inclined towards the revolutionaries, but it also gained politically from their schemes of action, while professing an ideology radically different and denigrating these forces. The repression provoked by the assassination attempts not only made a number of Indians more nationalist and thus pushed them towards the Congress, but what is more, the Party cashed in on the threat posed by the revolutionaries against the British. The latter found it expedient to make concessions to Gandhi and his men in an attempt to avoid inflating the numbers of the 'radicals'. Moreover, at the Round Table Conference in 1931 Gandhi declared to the British: 'if you know how to work with the Congress in the best possible way, you will bid adieu to terrorism'.[129] Kama Mclean pertinently points out that 'the presence of the revolutionaries on the political landscape during the crucial interwar years served to radicalise the Congress which, in turn, injected a fresh urgency into the slow British project of constitutional reform'.[130]

CONCLUSION

Analysing the place of the revolutionary repertoire in India, spanning nearly half a century, makes one understand a few changes and many constants.

The revolutionary repertoire has changed with time. Replete with religious references at the beginning of the twentieth century, it has become secular in the inter-war period. Purely nationalist, to begin with, it became, with time, progressively internationalist

[128] Ibid., p. 177.

[129] Cited by Peter Heehs, 'Terrorism and the National Movement', op.cit., p. 9.

[130] Kama Maclean, op. cit., pp. 20–21.

and proletarian (involving the workers and the peasants), while recognizing, little by little, the rifts, no longer only of classes but also of castes and religions.[131]

The man who epitomizes this transition is Bhagat Singh. His Janus-like appearance reflected his two sources of inspiration (Bolshevism and Anarchism), the Marxist one becoming dominant by the late 1920s. Bhagat Singh, who died when he was 23, was an exceptional person, as A.G. Noorani pointed out, because of his 'intellectual strength'.[132] But his evolution has been followed by others, including Shiv Verma, one of the founders of the HSRA. Verma, however, admitted in a 1986 article, that if in 1928 the firm resolution to turn away from 'anarchism and to make socialism an act of faith'[133] had been taken, 'in practice, we held on to our old style of individual actions':[134]

> It took us three years to realize the limitations of individual action. We moved towards socialism with measured steps, and it was only after our arrests that we had enough time and enough books to read, to discuss, to return to the past, and to arrive at the right conclusions.[135]

[131] Ashok Dhawale points out that 'The Hindi edition of *The Complete Works of Bhagat Singh* edited by Chaman Lal, comprises three very significant articles that were published in the Punjabi and Urdu monthly *Kirti* in May and June 1928. The titles of these three articles are: 'Religion and Our Freedom Struggle'; 'Communal Riots and their Solution'; and 'The Problem of Untouchability' (Ashok Dhawale, 'Shaheed Bhagat Singh: An Immortal Revolutionary', The Marxist, Volume XXII, No. 2–3, April-September 2006, p. 11). These titles are revealing of the attention that Bhagat Singh paid to caste and the relation between religion and politics.

[132] A.G. Noorani, *The Trial of Bhagat Singh – Politics of Justice*, New York, Oxford University Press, 2001.

[133] Shiv Verma, 'Ideological development of the revolutionary movement from Chapekars to Bhagat Singh', *in* Shiv Verma (ed.), *Bhagat Singh. On the Path to Liberation*, Chennai, Bharat Puthakalyam, 2007, p. 38.

[134] Ibid., p. 44.

[135] Ibid., p. 46.

But it was too late for the HSRA which had been decimated by repression since not only many leaders were arrested but others, like Bhagat Singh were executed or killed in an exchange of fire with the police, like Azad in 1931. It was not before the 1940s that the Communist Party of India was to fulfill Bhagat Singh's prophecy by taking up the cause of revolution not violently and clandestinely, but in the public sphere and on the basis of a proper organization.

The accumulation of the differences could make one doubt the existence of a revolutionary tradition in colonial India. This is however, proved by a few constants.

The first two generations of revolutionaries from Savarkar to Bhagat Singh primarily cultivate the same 'propaganda by action', even if the latter feels the need to form a political party towards the end of his life. This takes us back to our previous conclusion, and to a contradiction between theory and practices that Bipan Chandra has highlighted about the revolutionaries of the 1920s:

> Basically, their failure can be expressed in a series of contradictions between their ideology and their work. While in theory they were committed to socialism, in practice they could not go beyond nationalism. While in theory they desired mass action and mass struggle, in practice they could not rise above terrorist or individual action. While in theory they wanted to base their movement on the masses – the peasants and workers – in practice they could only appeal to the urban lower middle class or petty bourgeois youth. While in theory they wanted to create and lead a mass movement, in practice they remained a small band of heroic youth.[136]

Secondly, and more importantly, the question of violence is a vital thread which runs across the whole period under review

[136] Bipan Chandra, 'The Ideological Development of the Revolutionary Terrorists in Northern India in the 1920s', in *Nationalism and Colonialism in Modern India*, Hyderabad, Orient Longman, 1989.

and disturbed the revolutionaries in one way or the other. The problem is found everywhere, in all societies and in all ages. But in India it assumes acuteness greater than anywhere else because of the supreme value attached to the ideal of non-violence in Hinduism. In India, much of the charisma of Gandhi derived from this specific sensitivity. As a result, all the revolutionaries had to face the question of their relationship with violence and it is this query that unites them. The first generation, inspired by Tilak and Aurobindo, justified violence in Machiavellian terms (the end justifies the means) and at the same time took recourse to the religious justification that the Bhagavad Gita preaches: for certain Hindus taking recourse to violence is a sacred duty as long as the violent act is carried out in a spirit of renouncement, hence of sacrifice. For this first school, recourse to violence is indissociable from self-sacrifice, as the surrender of V.D. Savarkar and quite a few others stand witness to.

The second generation, especially from the time of Bhagat Singh, freed itself from all religious references, and, therefore, came up with another discourse on violence which however, remained loaded with denial. The notion of sacrifice remained central. To Gandhi, who reproached the revolutionaries for their 'cult of the bomb', Bhagat Singh objected that he did not wish to be murderous and that he died by sacrificing himself to atone for the shame attached to violent action. Violence is transcended in the sense that what is called 'violence' is not really so for the revolutionaries. Ultimately violence begets violence – first, of capitalist or feudal exploitation and/or of the State.

Today this denial of violence is still at the heart of a certain discourse of the Maoists. The dialogue between the then star anchor of *New Delhi Television* and the revolutionary minstrel Gadar is most eloquent:

> Sardesai: Gadar, is it true that the Naxals are now killing innocents with their violence?

> Gadar: Yeh violence nahin hota hai. Yeh aag hota hai [This is not violence. This is fire] (Starts singing) Aag hai, yeh aag hai/Yeh bhookey pet ki aag hai/Yeh aansuyon ki angaar hai/Yeh jangal ki lalkaar hai [This is a fire/Fire from empty bellies/The spark from tears/ The war cry of the jungle] (Stop singing) So the violence is of the sarkar [government]. The people are only retaliating. The state has become a terrorist .[137]

In the 1920s–1930s, the revolutionaries' rejection of violence made their ideology even more compatible with Gandhi's Congress. In fact, they were the two faces of the same freedom movement, the main difference coming from their view of socio-economic transformation.

This chapter covers up to the early 1930s, when the decimation of the HSRA sealed the fate of the second phase of the Indian revolutionary movement. A third phase took place in the 1940s with the rise of the Communists who implemented for the first time the revolutionary methods recommended by Bhagat Singh in terms of popular insurrection. This strategy culminated in the insurgency of Telengana in the late 1940s. But this movement stopped in 1951 as a result of the state's repression as of the change of strategy which the Communist Party of India opted for, namely, electoral competition within the framework of the newly established parliamentary system.

This shift calls to mind Lala Hardayal and M.N. Roy, both of whom had also renounced on the revolutionary option. Indeed, in India, to follow the revolutionary party line over years is an exception rather than the rule. But each time a communist party becomes more centrist, it opens a space for the Left and a new force appears in this vacuum. In the mid-1960s, the parliamentary path of the CPI favored the creation of the CPI(M) and in the late-1960s, the fact that the latter followed the same strategy

[137] Cited by Sudeep Chakravarti, op.cit., p. 191.

enabled a Maoist movement, the Naxalites, to take shape. Today the latter are the last revolutionaries.

GLOSSARY

Akharas: place of physical exercise traditionally attached to a Hindu temple.

Anushilan: Discipline, in the spiritual sense of the term.

Bhangis: untouchable caste, sweepers by profession.

Chamars: untouchable caste of cobblers and shoe-repairers.

Halal: food prepared for following Muslim rites/rituals.

Jhatka: food prepared following Hindu rites and dietary restrictions.

Jotedar: landlords of Bengal.

Kshatriya: warrior caste.

Naxalism: name of the Maoist movement in India which originated in the Naxalbari uprising in 1967.

Nizam: Name of the Muslim prince in the State of Hyderabad.

Sadhu: A Hindu who has renounced the pleasures of the world.

Shakta: Worshipper of shakti, a goddess (goddess Kali) of the Hindus.

Swadeshi: 'of the country by itself'. Movement of boycotting foreign products.

Yajna: Hindu sacrifice.

Lenin addressing his supporters in the October Revolution, 1917

Source: https://youronevoicecanmakeadifference.files.wordpress.com/2011/05/the-russian-revolution-1917-1923-also-known-as-the-october-revolution-led-by-vladimir-lenin.jpg

chapter 5

What is Revolution All About?

Postscript: Reflections

Hamit Bozarslan

Whether desired or feared, a revolution, as noted by Victor Hugo in his time,[1] is, above all, a tempest, a deep wave, pushing a society towards its future; it is simultaneously an active subject and a helpless spectator of its own destiny. It is equally an enigma, as each time it is spatial, temporal and yet universal. Hence the difficulty but also the necessity of a historical sociology of the act of revolution beyond exclusive confines of European experiences.

Let us begin with this 'Old Continent'. In his synthetic work, titled modestly *History of Revolutions*, Martin Malia, a renowned authority on the former regime of Russia and the Soviet Union[2], singles out a type of revolution that he defines as 'historically European'. For this ardent follower of François Furet who, furthermore, finds his source of inspiration in both Tocqueville and Weber, a 'European historical revolution' is determined by the internal contradictions of Europe, fragmented by the heritage of feudalism and yet unified by Christianity. The European world is largely stratified but is also wrought by a quest for legitimate equality by the discursive register and with a religious orientation.

[1] http://www.matierrevolution.fr/spip.php?article 602.

[2] Martin Malia, *Comprendre la Révolution russe*, Paris, Seuil, 1980.

According to Malia, it is religious dissidence, appearing in the form of heresy, which provides 'the initial momentum towards a radical change of society'. Whatever interpretation it gives to the sacred reference, a 'heresy' is, above all, a radical challenge to the world made of orders and hierarchy, of instances of power and direction. By the very dynamics that it triggers and the community practices that it introduces and imposes, it functions as a 'force of egalitarianism'[3].

Consequence of dogmatic controversies which are constituents of the Church, religious dissidence can extend itself beyond the serene surroundings of the abbey or the Bishop's house to lead to mass movements, give birth to the revolutionary, and if one is to follow the analysis of Malia, can mark the passage from the religion of salvation to axiology as the politics of salvation. The reason behind this burst of activity is simple: men of God who defect and join the dissidents, are only rarely in opposition to control egalitarian expectations, even millenarists, whom they incite by their new interpretations of religious reference. According to Malia, the egalitarian republic of Jan Huss in Prague (1419-20), the revolt of Thomas Münzer and other 'heretic' protests in Germany (1525–34) which gathered momentum from the Reform – though it associated them with the outward signs of Satan – constituted the most dramatic episodes of this search for liberation and for a new eschatology, as much religious as it was political.

'WEST-EAST GRADIENT'

We will not necessarily follow Malia in his approach to the 'singularization' of Europe; in any case, comparative studies of Christianity, the two other monotheisims and non-monotheist religions would be necessary to contradict or to confirm the hypothesis of the 'heresy' as source of revolutionary legitimacy

[3] *Ibid.*, p. 17 et suiv.

and mode of action, specifically Christian and European. We may, therefore, recall a number of insurrections or messianic Muslim[4] protests which present surprising parallels with the heresies or messianic movements of pre-modern Europe. For us, however, the true contribution of Malia to a historical sociology of the revolutions lies elsewhere, in his hypothesis of the existence of a European 'West-East gradient' which dates back to the rupture between Constantinople and Rome (1059). According to the American historian, whether they are a part of a religious dissidence or fall under a political or scientific banner, whether they are pre-modern or modern, the European historical revolutions indeed took place in the West from this quest before moving towards the East with the Russian Revolution between 1904 and 1917. This movement of decentralization equally corresponds to the universalization of the revolutionary phenomenon.

The chronology of the revolutionary episodes of global importance seems to prove this view: Teheran (1906), Istanbul (1908), Mexico (1910), Peking (1911) and, of course, Moscow (1917) take over from Petrograd in 1905. Unlike the revolts of the slaves against their masters, as those in Haiti (1791–1804), these uprisings (which, as in certain cases, as in the Ottoman Empire, take the form of a *pronunciamiento*) aim at bringing about a change of order, political and social, and pit a power and an armed opposition force, both 'indigenous' against one another. Almost at the same time as the triggering off of these uprisings – at times considered as the extension of the great French Revolution – one observes the great revolutions coming to an end in Europe itself.[5] Indeed, the Old Continent witnesses a number

[4] See, as an example, the special number of *REMMM* (no. 91–94, 2002) on the millenarianism of the Islamic world.

[5] Let us, however, remember here the importance of the three specific experiences of short duration in the wake of the First World War: the German Revolution of 1918, the Finnish insurrection of 1918 and the Hungarian Soviet Republic of 1919.

of radical movements taking place during the twentieth century but the existing political systems are able to integrate them and to supervise and control them by giving a central and visible place to their 'representatives' who have the double role of representing and controlling them. Similarly, in course of the first half of the 20th century, we witness brutal changes of regimes in Europe. Spain becomes the centre of a forceful restoration following a change over to democratic politics and the Portugal of Salazar proves that a conservative revolution is always possible in Europe. Following on with these ideas, and remembering Francois Furet, let us remember that Fascism and Nazism are both regimes born of revolutionary processes. But unlike the October Revolution, these four examples do not at all indicate an anticipation of a universal emancipation. If they serve as models for numerous movements of the Right in Europe or elsewhere[6], each asserts itself explicitly as the expression of a particular nation (defined as a species or as an organic body), at war with universalism (or, to use one of their favourite terms, against cosmopolitanism). The Revolutions of the Right reveal a universal phenomenon, that they do not enjoy the least pretension of being universal other than the brutal force of occupation they use.

The movement of displacement of expectation and the revolutionary phenomenon of Eastern Europe to the rest of the world (South America, Africa, Asia, Middle East) continues all along the 20th century, coming to the last big tidal wave in 1970 and finally resulting in the independence of Africa, the defeat of America in South East Asia, the Sandinista revolutions in Nicaragua and the Islamic Revolution in Iran. Except in Iran where Islamism wins over the Left, till now the initial starting point of the protest, the universal prestige earned by the revolutionary

[6] Stein Ugelvik Larsen (ed.), *Fascism outside Europe. The European Impulse against Domestic in the Diffusion of Fascism*, Boulder, Social Science Monographs, 2001.

idea, comes with the domination of the Left, introduced in the 'Marxist-Leninist' (or Maoist) form or of a paradoxical pairing of 'socialism' and a local reference (as 'Islamic socialism'). While 'coup d'État' becomes the term for the action of restoration of the Right all over the world, the very term, 'revolution' is associated, for the greater part of the century, with the Left.

WESTERNIZATION AND THE CENTRALITY OF THE INTELLIGENTSIA

The coupling of the revolution and the Left results as much in the process of Westernization as in the emergence all over the world of a particular class of people – the intelligentsia. Certainly, the rise to power of the Left signifies the end of Westernization as ideology, urging people to imitate the West resulting in a history – which was a synonym of corruption and moral degeneration – devoid of clarity. But what actually happens is that, based on the radical criticism of a model that establishes the domination of class as source of imitation and the global ascendancy of European (later American) 'imperialism' in the perspective of liberation, the Left is characterized as firmly rooted in the process of Westernization. Not only are its theoretical references or its vocabulary (imperialism, feudalism, proletariat ...) historically western, even its apprenticeship, its diffusion, the formulation of its local interpretations – all are made possible by the Westernization of those who may be called the elite intermediaries of the world.

The October Revolution, even the victory of 1945, which considerably enhances the prestige of the USSR, does not put a stop to this process. Indeed, Russian socialism is itself the product of a certain European historical context and even when the USSR gives to its communist allies generous study grants, the apprenticeship of 'Marxism-Leninism'continues to thrive through the intermediary – first the French, then the English and not the Russian. It is through these two languages that one is acquainted with the 'classics', and the *Elementary Principles of Philosophy* by Georges Politzer (1935) or the *ABCD of Socialism* by Leo Huberman (1962) does infinitely more to diffuse the ideas of the Left than the *Complete Works* of Lenin. This Russian intelligentsia which at the end of the 19th century, got familiarized with the German criticism of the 'French model', not by moving into and settling in Berlin or by taking help of German, a language known to be difficult, but with the help of the French translation of German writings[7]; the non-western world is initiated in the criticism of the liberal and capitalist model via the West and not the 'Red East'.

As for the intelligentsia, whose sociological profile has been studied in the Russian context by Franco Venturi and Martin Malia[8], it turns out, through decades, to be a phenomenon entirely universal. One sees it emerge, almost simultaneously, with its Russian counterpart, in the Balkan and Anatolian contexts at the turn of the 20th century[9]. One can detect its presence in the Chinese context in the period 1919–40 or again in the African in the decades 1950–70. This universalization of a particular sociological profile is not thought to be foreign to the Westernization of the elite intermediaries of the world who, even if they are not in power, nevertheless have at their disposal a unique cultural resource. From the Ottoman Empire to China (without even taking into account colonized India), the old systems of education were in favour of transmission of knowledge from teacher to student, paving the way, since the second half of the 19th century, for a new method of

[7] Alexandre Koyré, *La philosophie et le problème national en Russe an début du xix siècle*, Paris, Gallimard, 1976 (1re éd.: 1926).

[8] Franco Venturi, *Les intellectuels, le people et la révolution. Histoire du populisme russe au XX siècle*, Paris, Gallimard, 1972; Martin Malia, "What is Intelligentsia", *in* Richard Pipes (ed.), *The Russian Intelligentsia*, New York, Columbia University Press, 1961, pp. 1–18.

[9] See Hamit Bozarslan, "De l'action révolutionaire aux "bandes" au pouvoir: les comitadjilik ottomans au tournant du XX siècle", *in* Henry Laurens (ed.), *Typologies du terrorisme et communauté (-s) de valeurs*, Paris, CNRS Éditions, 2010, pp. 67–88.

education, based on experimental and critical knowledge, which is reviewed continuously. Whether they are military academies or medical schools, Ecole Normale or 'Technical Institutes of Agriculture', this knowledge plays a central role, often tragic, in rendering obsolete former titular figures like the well-read government officials in China, the teachers of Madrasas in the Ottoman countries or learned Africans[10].

The intelligentsia, product of a process of diffusion of a new method of teaching (and starting from a feeling of apprehension of the world) that, depending on the countries, continues till the end of the 1970s, becomes the spearhead of propagation of revolutionary ideas. It is indeed, the only social category who has the necessary cultural capital to formulate a criticism of the world and to produce a new political syntax, breaking away completely from existing systems. Formed, according to the local context, of children of the petty aristocracy, of the bourgeois traders, the clergy, the artisans or even the underprivileged section of society with gradual access to education, it (the intelligentsia) monopolises an encyclopaedic knowledge and controls the world with varied interpretations, which also includes applied technical knowledge, driving it along towards praxis. This knowledge which we shall describe as median and which is made popular to some extent, is always uncertain, since it necessitates a constant revision of the standard and an internal criticism. But it has nevertheless an integrated structure, indeed linear, in so far as it enables the increase of generalization, like the implementation of knowledge transfer on the nature (even in certain tragic cases, of the biology) of society.

Finally it can go well with a teleological mysticism that considers current times the bearer of corruption. This tool consequently becomes the instrument of suppression of this

[10] We shall read about it in the novel *La flèche de Dieu* (Paris, Présence Africaine, 1978) by Achebe Chinua, otherwise well analysed by Norbert Elias in *Le temps* (Paris, Pocket, 1999).

(current) time and imposition of a just time by exiting alienation and its inherent characteristics, notably class-based society and social backwardness caused by 'semi-feudalism' and 'imperialist domination'. It can, thanks to its cultural capital, interpret the world and transform it (The famous '11 Theses' of Marx!). The intelligentsia can equally legitimize the substitution of "criticism" of weapons to the weapon of criticism thanks to its force[11] and in the name of its 'conscience'.

Its force – since it constitutes a numerically important category – is in control of the administrative machinery of numerous sectors, from education to health, from civil engineering to law. In societies which remain predominantly rural before the 1980s, the small number of the working class only helps to make them socially visible in urban centres, and translates into building their own spaces for socialization. Its 'empowered' conscience, compared to its actual conditions, makes it think of itself as belonging to the oppressed classes, sharing their misery and predicting a future of emancipation. The Leninist model that separates the working class from its conscience, the one which would be represented by an avant-gardist elite and not by itself, reinforces the intelligentsia in this role, but at the cost of a solitary burden.

In reality it shares this burden. Its position of a social intermediary between the ruling elite and the 'people', its ability to translate its axiological knowledge in the form of slogans, not only allows it to mobilize the youth, its own source of reproduction as well as the women's movement, and those most deprived. It can form class alliances, though not introspective in the least, but nevertheless effective as testimony to the weight of mass organizations – organizations of workers and of peasants, in a good many revolutionary contexts, or simply long-term political mobilizations; this way, it becomes the principal intermediary of

[11] See Boris I. Kolonickij, "Les identities de l'intelligentsia russe et l'anti-intellectualisme", *Cahiers du monde russe*, 2002, n 4, vol.43, pp. 601–16.

social integration of a number of plebian actors and the common publicist of cultural capital.

To be able to succeed in the 'historic mission' that it targets, it should, indeed, remain at the same time an autonomous actor and accept its gradual decline as a historic agent in the course of the process named 'going to the people'. For a contemporary observer, the corner stone in the thought process of the intellectual workers and peasants, that strikes the historian, even in the context of the Naxalite movement in contemporary India[12], is that it brands itself as a producer of dissident political direction which goes much beyond its circles of socialization and militancy.

The intelligentsia takes the key role of inter-generational and inter-class action which mark a considerable part of the revolutionary protest movements all over the world[13]. Thus, the 'mindless' revolutionary of the intelligentsia, who occupies a very inconsequential place in intellectual history, can he actually constitute the hard core of a hegemonic political syntax, finding certainties in science as much as a horizon of liberation in faith?

These historical references, taken from a plurality of historical space and time make the analysis of the subject 'Marxism-Leninism' or even 'Maoism' extremely complex for the present day researcher. Can we, moreover, construct such a subject even as a research requirement? Nothing can be less certain. Nobody has any doubt today that the Soviet Union of Stalin (which whether we want to admit it or not, found its origins in Lenin) and the China of the Cultural Revolution, without even mentioning North Korea of Kim Il Sung, were totalitarian regimes. One would readily agree to define the socialist post-Stalinist regimes in the USSR, in Central Europe or even in Cuba, as authoritarian. Who can, moreover, deny that everywhere, where it was established, 'real socialism'

[12] See Laurent Gayer and Christophe Jaffrelot (eds.), *Milices armées d'Asie du Sud: privatization de la violence et implication des États*, Paris, Sciences Po, 2008.

[13] Theda Skocpol, *States and Social Revolutions. A Comprehensive Analysis of France, Russia and China*, Cambridge, Cambridge University Press, 1979, p. 18.

became synonymous with a system of bureaucratic domination, highly equalizing no doubt, but also strongly repressive? If socialist experiences elsewhere in the world from the Red Aden to the Ethiopia of Mengistu Haile Maryam, did not lack the material means to allow themselves a certain degree of bureaucratization, they were no less equalizing nor repressive. Meanwhile, on the reverse side, from Allende's Chile to Turkey of the 1960s, numerous areas emerged where 'Marxism-Leninism', if not socialism, became a search for liberation and massive political mobilization. Likewise, in a number of cases, dissidents belonging to the Left refused the option of revolutionary violence, and asserted their rights, often at their own risk, through the electoral process, often blocked by the pressure of bourgeois democracies. Without this articulation with social struggles not found in the works of Furet (and of Malia), it will be difficult to understand the meaning of the Left in countries where they won without taking up arms.

WAR AS CONSTRUCTION OF REVOLUTIONARY POWER

The period post-1917 also leads to another change of global magnitude. While becoming a means of seizing power or associating it with a resistance of long duration, the revolution ceases to be synonymous with the 'big eve' of revolt. But it still does not succeed unless there is a breakdown. As an example, the Kemalist movement considered its War of Independence from 1919 to 1922 (which adds to its Eastern frontier a devastating war against the new Armenian republic, already weakened by the genocide of 1915 and, internally, to a policy of ethnic cleansing against the Greeks of Anatolia), as the revolutionary phase of its history, justifying the installation of a regime, made to appear explicitly revolutionary. The war not only against the external 'enemies', but also internal (notably the 'traitors'), was apprehended as violence, laying the foundation of a new regime born out of *a tabula rasa.* The discourse of Mustafa Kemal in 1927, pronounced after the physical elimination or marginalization of his former companions following the same path, will end the phase of the Revolution as such to begin a revolutionary regime which, with time, would be looked as one of the three pillars of a new non-liberal world along with fascist Italy and the Soviet Union.

Deeply nationalist, Kemalism was not, in any way, a movement of the Left. In a number of cases, as in China, Laos, Vietnam, or even in Africa, the anti-colonial or anti-imperialist, armed struggle served as a substitute to the phase of open rebellion and allowed the building of an army and a new revolutionary political power of the Left. With the same radicalism as the French, Russian, or even the Iranian Revolutions, these military resistances effectively eliminated their 'former regimes' to project themselves in future, starting from the imaginary *tabula rasa*, showing that power depended in the last instance on the 'end of the gun', giving rise to systems, that were egalitarian yet repressive. One finds that this unusual revolutionary trajectory becomes a source of inspiration to challenges in contexts other than the anti-colonial or the anti-imperialist War; Maoism, notably, becomes necessary as a revolutionary reference, largely autonomous, for a number of protest movements in societies, either non-colonized or postcolonial, from the Peru of the *Shining Path* to the Turkey of the 1970s, stirred up by half a dozen organizations, from Nepal to India, to followers of Mazumdar in the years 1990 to 2000. In reality the victory of the partisan war as revolution aroused huge expectations beyond the effective exit of Maoist China in the second half of the 70s, or the great transformations at the turn of the decade of 1990.

CONSTRUCTION OF THE PARTICULAR THROUGH THE UNIVERSAL

In an article which has already become dated, Jean Leca has underlined an important paradox, one associated with the

French Revolution and relevant to revolutions in general: that a revolution takes place by an uprising or by a deeply rooted and continuous armed struggle whereby the universal constructs the particular,[14] enabling it to establish itself as subject of history, transcending its fate, explained by a universal condition and its sufferings for consenting humanity in general. Leca recalls in this context the slogan of the Algerian moujahadi: 'While fighting against you, we shall liberate you and liberate ourselves'. In a sense, each particular warring group is considered as an 'elected' group of people whose emancipation is the human condition as a whole and, consequently, also of its executioners. Leca's explanation has a strong analytical power for the understanding of the propagation of the ideas of the Left in what was formerly called the Third World (and without doubt beyond it). In reality, commitment towards the Left often makes it possible for an ethnic and sectarian community to distance itself from a colonial power or from a dominantly sectarian group. Such a positioning in the political spectrum and, following on from history in the process of construction of the future, is not therefore without consequence for the evolution of these groups, radically reconfigured by the new meaning and form of militancy, where new hierarchies find their principal source of legitimization.

On the other hand, one can come to the hypothesis that, to become audible and to be locally accepted, the Left had to, often in a non-instrumental manner, mobilise local, cultural and religious resources like Hinduism or the 'Christian mechanisms' of post-Columbian societies, discussed respectively in this volume by Christoffe Jaffrelot and Gilles Bataillon. Likewise, everywhere in the non-European world (and even in certain European countries like France or Italy), the revolutionary protest movement seized the question of independence either formulated as an anti-colonial struggle or as emancipation in relation to the United States, and

[14] "Nationalisme et Universalisme", *Pouvoirs*, n 57, 1991, pp. 32–42.

overcame the standard apprehensions of the Left with regard to the national question.

This fact is particularly noticeable within the minority communities. We have already emphasized, in the chapter dealing with the Middle East, the quasi-hegemonical impact of the left among the Kurds and the Palestinians, where a number of intellectuals and militants were seduced by the principle of the right of the people to self-determination preached by 'Marxism-Leninism'. This horizon of national liberation was equally considered as the condition of a fraternity of the dominant groups in the direction where their national liberation should lead the 'oppressor class' to free itself of its own mechanisms of oppression. In the forced marriage imposed by the 'tormentors of the oppressor class' that condemned them to occupy a marginal place in history, unions of consenting people and classes, earlier oppressed, and now rid of their enemies are suddenly catapulted in front of this history. This game of discrimination among the minorities in relation to dominant ethnic groups could, moreover, recur within the 'Family of the Left'. For example, in Sri Lanka, Trotskyism became the trademark of the protest movement of the Tamil minority (group) against the Stalinist 'Marxism', already monopolized by the youth of the dominant group[15].

The sectarian minority groups were equally sensitive to the speeches of liberation of the Left. In Iraq, not only the communist movement (but also at least at the initial stage, the 'Socialist' Ba'ath party which was going to become extremely anti-Shiiite under the rule of Saddam Hussain, for instance, during the period 1979–2003) drew, in the decades 1940-60, on this community. Notwithstanding the criticisms that the Communist Party had reserved for religion (and not exclusively for Islam) as much as a system of religious faith and 'superstructure' of the power

[15] Donald L. Horowitz, *Ethnic Groups in Conflict*, Berkeley, Los Angeles-London, University of California Press, 1985, p. 10, 336–37.

relationships of class society, 'Communism'could easily make sense in the Shi'ite context, elaborately practiced over years since its origins with a millenarist expectation. Indeed it enabled the transition from a religious to a political eschatology, redefining the very idea of liberation and proposing new modes of action to achieve it. The same applies to Alévis in Turkey, very sensitive to the message of the radical Left and at the same time in tune with a political culture, replete with anti-establishment themes and appropriate for an esoteric language in the sense in which Koyré employed the term[16].

But the Left at the same time offered them new ways of interpreting the repression they suffered in the period 1960–70, while it simultaneously experimented with a rapid urbanization and dissolution of their traditional solidarity. The Alévis militants could consequently legitimize their commitment to the Left by their own mythology of resistance against oppression to explain their status as victim through sufferings endured in the name of humanity and to project themselves in future as actors of human liberation outside the community of the Alévis.

RETURN TO EUROPE

Twenty years after the disappearance of the Soviet Union, 'Marxism-Leninism' (and its Maoist variant) appears as a double subject of interrogation. If, on the one hand, there is no doubt that it transformed itself into an illusion, a complete utopia, where a simple human intervention would be the condition of the teleological exit of alienation, on the other hand, it offered to

[16] 'If war, from an exceptional state became a situation, perpetual and normal [...], the lie in an exceptional case would itself become normal [...]. A social group which would find itself and feel surrounded by enemies, would never hesitate to use the lie against them. Truth, for them, untruth for the others, would become a code of conduct, would enter the mores of the group in question' Alexandre Koyré, *Réflexions sur le mensonge*, Paris, Alia, 1998, p. 22

the marginalized and subordinate groups, answers to understand their conditions and fight the power relationships of which they were victims. The two versions of Opposition to liberation, one in the Soviet Union and the other in China, gave birth elsewhere to discourses and to struggles for liberation in the context of repression.

Indeed, one cannot deny the reality and cruelty of these power relationships, or forget that in more cases than one, the simplest evocation of socialism, even of the social question, triggered atrocities and coercive policies, patronized by the United States, which elaborated the doctrine. The repression of the Left, accompanied massacre of opponents in a number of countries, from Indonesia in the 1960s to Chile or Argentina in the 1970s, did not only expose the contradictions between the discourse of the bourgeois state and its praxis that Furet analyses in his work; it also forced the Left to militarize itself, to sanctify the memory of its fighters and to pledge fidelity and vengeance, transforming commitment into a calling, and reproducing, in turn, Carl Schmitt's vision of politics, seen as an arena of struggle between friends and foes.

If the historian is aware of the risks of retrospective 'political fiction' as a speculative exercise, he cannot, however, refrain from thinking that without the authoritarianism of the pro-Western rcgimcs and without the logic of the Cold War that, in a large number of countries, was perfectly 'Hot', and the trajectory followed by the radical Left could have been different on the global political scene. The memoirs of Hans-Joachim Klein, former militant of the *Red Army Faction*, or the writings of Donatella della Porta on Germany and Italy[17], demonstrate very well how this group was, in fact, in search for integration in the political

[17] Hans-Joachim Klein, *La mort mercenaire. Témoignage d'un ancient terroriste ouest-allemand*, Paris, Le Seuil, 1980; Donatella della Porta, *Social Movements, Political Violence and the State: A Comparative Analysis of Italy and Germany*, Cambridge University Press, 1995.

systems, its potential tendency to take the path of violence getting reduced as it became firmly established.

Finally, comes the question of the usefulness of being acquainted with these non-Western experiences to understand the revolutionary passions of West Europe. The specific question goes beyond that of the legitimacy of the comparative exercise which remains heuristically rich. Following the argument of Martin Malia, we will readily accept that 1917 constitutes a key date not only because of the October Revolution, but also as a major landmark in the shift of the revolutionary phenomenon to the East of the 'Gradient West-East'. For Western Europe, this shift seems to have signified a long-term separation of direct revolutionary experience and pro-revolutionary commitment. There is absolutely no doubt that the latter took the form of an 'illusion' and led to the suspension of critical reason with regard to 'real socialisms'. One cannot otherwise explain the blindness of the European Left about the deeply repressive experiences of the USSR or of China. But the argument also admits that, beyond the illusion, the available sources of inspiration in Europe, even to criticize bourgeois society, henceforth came from elsewhere. Uniting the people 'oppressed by the West' and the 'oppressed classes' of the West under condition of emancipation of the entire mankind, the 'call' from the South could only give rise to strong and loud echoes in the West, give birth to a surge of solidarity, to a willingness to escape the 'bourgeois state' responsible for an unequal world, and to instigate a desperate urgency to share the sacrifices of an 'elsewhere', thereby paying a heavy price in its quest for liberation.

The detour through the non-Western world also prompts one to ask other questions: to what extent can one compare the intelligentsia within the European framework with the rest of the world, where the intellectual emerged as a guardian, from his 'oppressor class' and that of the 'organic' intellectual of Gramsci, rooted, for his part, in the struggle for his 'oppressed class', and which of these categories dominated ? What were the links between the action of the intellectuals, fooled by an 'illusion' and the actual struggles whether social, political or even feminist ? Can one establish a link between the expectations of eschatological freedom and social liberation after the 'historic revolutions of Europe' that Malia talks about? Would certain minority groups, religious and linguistic (it is enough to mention the cases of Ireland and the Basque countries) provide privileged terrain for left militancy or, on a wider scale, the ideas of the Left interpreted as the road to universal emancipation, including their own?

So many questions remain which necessitate monographs and comparative studies, that should intervene to improve the current benchmark of analysis of the revolutionary passions in Europe.

Bibliography

Adenwalla Minoo, "Hindu concepts and the Gita in early Indian thought", *in* Robert A. Sakai (ed.), *Studies on Asia,* Lincoln, University of Nebraska Press, 1961.

Aflaq Michel, *Choix des textes de la pensée du fondateur du parti Ba'ath. Unité-Liberté-Socialisme,* Madrid, s.n., 1977.

Ahmad Djâlal al-e, *L'occidentalite,* Paris, L'Harmattan, 1988.

Alaniz Pinell Jorge, *Nicaragua, una revolucion reaccionaria,* Panama, Kosmos-Editorial S. A., 1985.

Al-Haj Saleh Yassin, "L'univers des anciens prisonniers politiques en Syrie", *REMMM,* n°s 115–116, 2007, pp. 249–65.

Anderson Charles W., *Political and Economical Change in Latin America,* Princeton, D. Van Nostrand Company Inc., 1967; traduction espagnole: *Cambio Politico y Economico en la America Latina,* Mexico Fondo de Cultura economica, 1974.

Annino Antonio, *Dall'insurrezione al regime. Politiche di massa e strzategie istituzionali a Cuba 1953–1965,* Milan, Franco Angeli Editore, 1984.

——— "La réforme agraire et le communisme à Cuba", *Communisme,* n°s 85–86, Paris, L'Âge d'Homme, 2006, pp. 65–83.

Arendt Hannah, *Essai sur la révolution,* Paris, Gallimard, 1967.

——— *Les origines du totalitarisme.Impérialisme,* Paris, Le Seuil, 1984.

Aurobindo Sri, *Bankim, Tilak, Dayanand,* Delhi, Sarvadeshik Arya Pratinidhi Sabha, 1984.

Avendano Rojas Xiomara, *Elecciones Indirectas y Disputa de Poder en Nicaragua: el lento camino hacia la modernidad,* Managua, Grupo editorial Lea, 2007.

Bataillon Gilles, "De Sandino aux *contras*. Formes et pratiques de la guerre au Nicaragua", *Annales,* n° 3, 60e année, mai-juin 2005, pp. 653–88.

——— *Genèses des guerres internes en Amérique centrale (1960–1983),* Paris, Les Belles Lettres, 2003.

Belli Giaconda, *El Pais bajo de mi piel,* New York, Vintage Books, 2002.

Bénichou Paul, *Le temps des prophètes. Doctrine de l'âge romantique,* Paris, Gallimard, 1977, coll. "Nrf".

Bennani-Chraibi Mounia et Olivier Fillieule (eds.), *Résistances et protestations dans les sociétés musulmanes,* Paris, Sciences Po, 2003.

Benounna Mehdi, *Héros sans gloire. Échec d'une révolution: 1963–1973,* Casablanca, Tarek Editions, 2002.

Berger Peter L., *Invitation to Sociology. A Humanistic Perspective,* New York-London-Toronto, Anchor Books, 1994.

Biardeau Madeleine, "Introduction", *Le Mahabharata,* Paris, Garnier-Flammarion, vol. 1, 1985.

Blunt Wilfrid Scawen, *My diaries Being a personal narrative of events, 1888–1914,* London, 1914.

Bourricaud François, "Dictadura, dictablanda et la question de l'hégémonie en Amérique du Sud", *in* Léo Hamon, *La fin des dictatures,* Paris, Economica, 1983.

Bozarslan Hamit, "Allemagne ou France: dualités ottomanes et problème des modèles", *CEMOTI,* n° 12, 1991, pp. 71–98.

——— "De l'action révolutionnaire aux "bandes" au pouvoir: les comitadjilik ottomans au tournant du xxe siècle", *in* Henry Laurens (ed.), *Typologies du terrorisme et communauté(s) de valeurs,* Paris, CNRS Éditions, 2010, pp. 67–88.

Brown Emily C., *Har Dayal: Hindu Revolutionary and Rationalist,* The University of Arizona Press, 1975.

Chabrier Édith, "Les délégués du Premier Congrès des Peuples d'Orient, Bakou (1er-8 septembre 1920)", *Cahiers du monde russe et soviétique,* vol. 26, 1985, pp. 21–42.

Chakravarti Sudeep, *Red sun. Travels in Naxalite country,* New Delhi, Penguin, 2008.

Charney Jean-Paul, *Principes de stratégie arabe,* Paris, L'Herne, 2003.

Chatterji Bankim Chandra, *Le monastère de la félicité,* Paris, Presse Orientalistes de France, 2003.

Cherem Silvia, *Una vida por la palabra. Entrevista con Sergio Ramirez,* Mexico, Fondo de Cultura Economica, 2004.

Chinua Achebe, *La flèche de Dieu,* Paris, Présence Africaine, 1978.

Chirol Valentine, *Indian Unrest*, London, Macmillan, 1910.

Christian Shirley, *Nicaragua Revolution in the Family,* New York, Random House, 1985.

Dalton Dennis, "The Gandhian view of caste and caste after Gandhi", *in* Philip Mason (ed.), *India and Ceylon: unity and diversity,* London-New York, Oxford University Press, 1967.

DeFronzo Jim, *Revolutionary Movements in World History. From 1750 to the Present*, Santa Barbara, ABC Clio, 2006, 3 vol.

Della Porta Donatella, *Social Movements, Political Violence and the State A Comparative Analysis of Italy and Germany,* Cambridge, Cambridge University Press, 1995.

Draper Theodore, "Le Castrisme", in *De Marx à Mao Tsé Toung*, Paris, Calmann-Lévy, 1967.

Duboc Marie, "Activism from the margins: overcoming the mobilisation/demobilisation dichotomy. A study of Left-Wing intellectuals in Egypt", unpublished article.

Dumont René, *Cuba est-il socialiste ?* Paris, Le Seuil, 1970.

——— *Cuba. Socialisme et développement,* Paris, Le Seuil, 1964.

——— *Finis les lendemains qui chantent,* Paris, Le Seuil, 1983.

Engels Friderich et Karl Marx, *L'idéologie allemande,* Paris, Éditions sociales, 1974.

Fanon Franz, *Pour la révolution africaine Écrits politiques,* Paris, La Découverte, 2006.

Foucault Michel, *Dits et écrits,* Paris, Gallimard, 1994, coll. "Nrf", vol. 3, pp. 746–47.

Franda Marcus F., *Radical Politics in West Bengal,* Cambridge Mass., The MIT Press, 1971.

Franqui Carlos, *Retrato de familia con Fidel,* Barcelone, Seix Barral, 1981.

Furet François, *L'atelier de l'histoire,* Paris, Flammarion, 1982.

——— "Préface", *in* Élie Halévy, *Correspondance, 1891–1937*, Paris, Fallois, 1996.

——— *La Révolution française*, Paris, Gallimard, 2007.

——— *Penser le xxe siècle*, Paris, Robert Laffont, 2007.

——— et Mona Ozouf (eds.), *Dictionnaire critique de la Révolution française,* Paris, Flammarion, 1988.

——— and Ran Halévy, "Préface", *Orateurs de la Révolution française,* vol. 1: *Les constituants,* Paris, Gallimard, 1989.

Furet François and Françoise Mélonio, «Préface», *in* A. de Tocqueville, *Œuvres,* Paris, Gallimard, 2004, coll. "Nrf", vol. 3.

Gayer Laurent et Christophe Jaffrelot (eds.), *Milices armées d'Asie du Sud: privatisation de la violence et implication des États,* Paris, Sciences Po, 2008.

Geertz Clifford, «Ideology as a Cultural System», *in* David Apter (ed.), *Ideology and Discontent,* New York, The Free Press, 1964.

Gandhi Mohandas Karamchand, *Indian Home Rule,* Madras, Ganesh, 1922.

——— *The traditional roots of charisma,* Chicago, The University of Chicago Press, 1983.

Ghodke H. M., *Revolutionary nationalism in Western India,* New Delhi, Classical Publishing House, 1990.

Ghosh Ajoy, *Articles and speeches*, Moscow, Publishing House for Oriental Literature, 1962.

Gökalp Z., *Yeni Hayat, Dogru Yol*, Ankara, M. E. B. Yayinlari, 1976, pp. 13–14.

Gopal Thakur, *Bhagat Singh. The man and his ideas*, New Delhi, 1976.

Gordon Leonard A., "Portrait of a Bengali revolutionary", *Journal of Asian Studies,* vol. 27, n° 2, 1968.

Graff Violette, *Les partis communistes indiens,* Paris, Presses de la FNSP, 1975.

Gros Frédéric, *États de violence: essai sur la fin de la guerre,* Paris, Gallimard, 2005.

Guillemarre-Acet Dorothée, *L'Allemagne, l'Empire ottoman et la Turquie républicaine: relations politiques et liens culturels (1908–1933),* Doctoral thesis of INALCO under the supervision of François Georgeon.

Habib S. Irfan, *To make the deaf hear. Ideology and programme of Bhagat Singh and his comrades,* Gurgaon, Three Essays, 2007.

Haffner Sebastian, *Histoire d'un Allemand. Souvenirs 1914–33,* Arles, Actes Sud, 2002.

Halévy Ran, *L'expérience du passé. François Furet dans l'atelier de l'histoire,* Paris, Gallimard, 2007.

Halliday Fred, *Arabia without Sultans*, London, Penguin, 1974.

Harrison Selig S., *The Most Dangerous Decades,* Princeton (NJ), Princeton University Press, 1960.

Hassner Pierre, "François Furet et le libéralisme mélancolique", *in* François Furet, *Penser le XXe siècle* (voir *infra*), pp. ix–xxiii.

——— *La revanche des passions,* Paris, Société des amis de François Furet, 2004.

Heehs Peter, *Nationalism, Terrorism, Communalism. Essays in Modern Indian History,* Delhi-New York, Oxford University Press, 1998.

Hirschman Alfred O., *Défection et prise de parole: théorie et application,* Paris, Fayard, 2005.

Hoda Noorul, *The Alipore bomb case. A historic pre-independence trial,* New Delhi, Niyogi Books, 2008.

Höpp Gerhard, *Mufti Papiren, Briefe, Memoranden, Reden und Anrufe Amin al-Husseinis aus dem Exil,* Berlin, Schiller Verlag, 2002.

Horowitz Donald L., *Ethnic Groups in Conflict,* Berkeley-Los Angeles-London, University of California Press, 1985.

Inalco, *L'expérience soviétique et le problème national dans le monde, 1920–1939*, Paris, Langues'O, 1981, 2 vol.

Iyengar K. R. Srinivasa, *Sri Aurobindo: A Biography and a History,* Pondichéry, Sri Aurobindo Ashram/SABDA, 1985, 4th edition, enlarged (Calcutta, Arya Publishing House, 1945).

Jaffrelot Christophe, *La démocratie par la caste. Histoire d'une mutation socio-politique (1885–2005),* Paris, Fayard, 2005.

——— *Ambedkar, leader intouchable et père de la Constitution indienne,* Paris, Presses de Sciences Po, 2000.

Jankowski James and Israel Gershomi (eds.), *Rethinking Nationalism in the Arab Middle East,* New York, Columbia University Press, 1997.

Jog Narayan Gopal, *Lokamanya Bal Gangadhar Tilak,* New Delhi, Ministry of Information & Broadcasting, 1979.

Jones Kenneth, *Socio-religious reform movements in British India,* Cambridge, Cambridge University Press, 1989.

Joshi Puran Chandra and K. Damodaran (eds.), *Marx comes to India,* Delhi, Manohar, 1975.

Karol Kewes S., *Les guérilleros au pouvoir,* Paris, Robert Laffont, 1970.

Ker James Campbell, *Political trouble in India: 1907–1917,* Calcutta, 1973 [1917].

Khoury Philip, "The Paradoxical Arab Nationalism: Interwar Syria Revisited", *in* James Jankowski and Israel Gershomi, *Rethinking*

Nationalism in the Arab Middle East, New York, Columbia University Press, 1997, p. 277.

Klein Hans-Joachim, *La mort mercenaire. Témoignage d'un ancien terroriste ouest-allemand,* Paris, Le Seuil, 1980.

Kolonickij Boris I., "Les identités de l'intelligentsia russe et l'anti-intellectualisme", *Cahiers du monde russe,* 2002, n° 4, vol. 43, pp. 601–16.

Koury Enver M., *The Patterns of Mass Movements in Arab Revolutionary Progressive States,* La Haye, Mouton, 1970.

Koyré Alexandre, *Réflexions sur le mensonge,* Paris, Alia, 1998.

Koyré Alexandre, *La philosophie et le problème national en Russie au début du xixe siècle,* Paris, Gallimard, 1976 (1st Edition: 1926).

Kutschera Chris (ed.), *Le Livre noir de Saddam Hussein,* Paris, Oh! Éditions, 2005.

Lanternari Vittorio, *Les mouvements religieux des peuples opprimés,* Paris, La Découverte, 1983.

Larsen Stein Ugelvik, (ed.), *Fascism Outside Europe. The European Impulse against Domestic in the Diffusion of Global Fascism,* Boulder, Social Science Monographs, 2001.

Laushey, David, *Bengal Terrorism and the Marxist Left. Aspects of Regional Nationalism in India, 1905–1942*, Calcutta, Firma K. L. Mukhopadhyaya, 1975, p. 34.

Lavau Georges, *À quoi sert le Parti communiste français ?* Paris, Fayard, 1981.

Leca Jean, "Nationalisme et Universalisme", *Pouvoirs,* n° 57, 1991, pp. 32–42.

Lefort Claude, *Un homme en trop,* Paris, Le Seuil, 1976.

——— "Esquisse d'une genèse de l'idéologie dans les sociétés modernes", in *Les formes de l'histoire,* Paris, Gallimard, 1978.

——— *La complication,* Paris, Fayard, 1999.

——— *Essais sur le politique XIXe-XXe siècles,* Paris, Le Seuil, 1986.

Leveau Rémy, "Vers une fonction tribunicienne", *in* Serge Cordelier (ed.), *L'Islamisme,* Paris, La Découverte, 1994, pp. 57–65.

Lewis Bernard, *Le retour de l'Islam,* Paris, Gallimard, 1985, coll. "Nrf".

——— *Le langage politique de l'Islam,* Paris, Gallimard, 1988, coll. "Nrf".

Maclean Karen, *A Revolutionary History of Interwar India*, London, Hurst, 2015, p. 231.

Malamoud Charles, "Le jeûne du créancier", *in* Louis Renou (ed.), *L'Inde fondamentale,* Paris, Hermann, 1978, pp. 164–74.

Malia Martin, "What is Intelligentsia", *in* Richard Pipes (ed.), *The Russian Intelligentsia,* New York, Columbia University Press, 1961, pp. 1–18.

——— *Comprendre la Révolution russe*, Paris, Seuil, 1980.

——— *Histoire des révolutions,* Paris, Tallandier, 2008.

Mannheim Karl, *Idéologie et utopie*, Paris, Éditions de la MSH, 2006.

Martinez-Gros Gabriel, *Ibn Khaldoun et les sept vies de l'Islam,* Arles, Actes Sud, 2006.

Massouilié François, *Les Conflits du Proche-Orient XXe siècle,* Paris, Casterman-Giunti, 1994.

Matos Hubert, *Como llego la Noche,* Barcelone, Tusquets, 2002; French translation: *Et la nuit est tombée*, Paris, Les Belles Lettres, 2006.

Meriç Cemil, *Magaradikler,* Istanbul, Ötüken Yayinlari, 1980.

Moghith Anwar, "Marxisme égyptien et marxisme occidental: traduction et idéologie", *Égypte Monde Arabe*, n°s 30–31, 1997, pp. 71–91.

Monciaud Didier (ed.), *Cahiers d'histoire Revue d'histoire critique,* numéros consacrés aux "Gauches en Égypte, xixe-xxe siècles", n°s 105–06, 2008.

Montenegro Sofia, "Es revolucionario el FSLN? El Nuevo Amanecer Cultural", *El Nuevo Diario,* Managua, 14 mai 1994.

——— "La "Hérotica" nacional masculina", *Debate Feminista,* avril 1999, vol. 19, n° 10, pp. 223–27.

Morales Moisés Hassan, *La maldicion del Guëguense,* Managua, 2009.

Mukherjee Haridas and Uma Mukherjee, "The alleged uniqueness of India's freedom movement", *Modern Review,* n° 112, 1962, pp. 106–07.

Muñoz Molina Antonio, *Séfarade,* Paris, Le Seuil, 2003.

Muzzafar Ahmed, *Communist Party of India Years of formation (1921–1933),* Calcutta, National Book Agency Private Ltd., 1959.

Nanda B. R., *Gandhi and Religion,* New Delhi, Oxford University Press, 1990.

Nandy Ashis, *At the Edge of Psychology: Essays in Politics and Culture,* Delhi-Oxford, Oxford University Press, 1980.

Nargolkar Vasant, *JP's Crusade for Revolution,* New Delhi, S. Chand, 1975.

Nichanian Marc, *Entre l'art et le témoignage Littérature arménienne du XXe siècle*, Paris, Metis Press, 2006–08.

Noorani, AG, *The Trial of Bhagat Singh – Politics of Justice*, New York, Oxford University Press, 2001.

Ostergaard Geoffrey, *Nonviolent Revolution in India,* New Delhi, Gandhi Peace Foundation, 1985.

Ozouf Mona, "François Furet, comment écrire la révolution", *in* François Furet, *La Révolution française* (cf. *infra*), pp. i–xxvi.

Paz Octavio, "America latina y la democracia", *Tiempo nublado,* Barcelona, Seix Barral, 1983; traduction française: "L'Amérique latine et la démocratie", in *Une planète pour quatre ou cinq mondes,* Paris, Gallimard, 1985, coll. "Folio-essais".

Pécaut Daniel, *L'ordre et la violence, évolution socio-politique de la Colombie entre 1930 et 1953,* Paris, Éditions de l'EHESS, 1987.

Ram Mohan, "The Communist movement in India", *in* Kathleen Gough and Hari P. Sharma (eds.), *Imperialism and Revolution in South Asia*, New York-London, Monthly Review Press, 1973.

Ramirez Sergio, *Adios Muchachos. Una memoria de la revolucion sandinista,* Mexico, Aguilar, 1999.

Ray Rabindra, *The Naxalites and Their Ideology,* Delhi, Oxford University Press, 1992 [1988].

Revel Jacques (ed.), *Jeux d'échelles. La micro-analyse à l'expérience,* Paris, Gallimard-Le Seuil-Éditions de l'EHESS, 1998, coll. "Hautes Études".

Richard Yann, *L'Iran. Naissance d'une république islamique,* Paris, La Martinière, 2006.

Rodinson Maxime, *Marxisme et le monde musulman,* Paris, Le Seuil, 1972.

——— *L'Islam politique et croyance,* Paris, Fayard, 1993.

Rosselli John, "The self-image of effeteness: physical education and nationalism in nineteenth century Bengal", *Past and Present,* 86, 1980.

Roussillon Alain, *Identité et modernité: les voyageurs égyptiens au Japon (XIXe-XXe siècles)*, Paris, Sindbad, 2005.

Rudolph Lloyd I. and Susanne H. Rudolph, *The Modernity of Tradition: Political Development in India,* Chicago, The University of Chicago Press, 1967.

Salamé Ghassan (ed.), *Démocraties sans démocrates. Politiques d'ouverture dans le monde arabe et islamique,* Paris, Fayard, 1994.

Sanabria Octavio et Elvyra Sanabria, *Nicaragua: Diagnostico de una traicion. El Frente Sandinista de Liberacion Nacional en el poder,* Barcelona, Plaza & Janes Editores, 1986.

Skocpol Theda, *States and Social Revolutions: A Comprehensive Analysis of France, Russia and China*, Cambridge, Cambridge University Press, 1979.

Scott James C., *La domination et les arts de la résistance: fragments du discours subalterne,* Paris, Éditions Amsterdam, 2009.

Schulze Reinhard, *A Modern History of Islamic World,* New York, New York University Press, 2002.

Singh Prakash, *Histoire du Naxalisme. Jacqueries et guérillas de l'Inde (1967–2003),* Paris, Les nuits rouges, 2004.

Sluglett Peter, "Le Parti Ba'ath: Panarabisme, national-socialisme et dictature", *in* Chris Kutschera, *Le Livre noir de Saddam Hussein,* Paris, Oh! Éditions, 2005.

Soljenitsine Alexander, *L'archipel du Goulag,* Paris, Le Seuil, 1976.

Sorel George, *Réflexions sur la violence,* Paris, Quartier Libre, 2006.

Srinivas Mysore Narasimhachar, "Gandhi's religion", *Economic & Political Weekly*, 24 June 1995, p. 1490.

Sternhell Zeev, *La droite révolutionnaire. Les origines françaises du fascisme: 1885–1914,* Paris, Le Seuil, 1984.

Szulc Tad, *Fidel a Critical Portrait,* New York, William Morrow and Company, 1986; French translation, *Castro, trente ans de pouvoir absolu*, Paris, Payot, 1987.

Tchakhotine Serguëi, *Le viol des foules par la propagande politique,* Paris, Gallimard, 1939.

Ter Minassian Talinn, *Colporteurs du Komintern: l'Union soviétique et les minorités au Moyen-Orient,* Paris, Sciences Po, 1997.

Thakur Gopal, *Bhagat Singh: The Man and His Ideas,* New Delhi, 1976.

Thomas Hugh, *Cuba: The Pursuit of Freedom,* New York, Harper and Row, 1971.

Tilak Bal Gangadhar, *Srimad Bhagavadgita-Rahasya or Karma Yoga Shastra,* Poona, 1965 [1936].

Tilly Charles, *Les révolutions européennes*, Paris, Le Seuil, 1993.

——— *The Politics of Collective Violence,* Cambridge-London, Cambridge University Press, 2003.

Traverso Enzo, "Le siècle de Hobsbawm", *La Revue internationale des livres et des idées*, n° 10, 2009.

Uways Sayyid, *L'histoire que je porte sur le dos...*, Marseille, Parenthèses, 2006.

Venturi Franco, *Les intellectuels, le people et la révolution. Histoire du populisme russe au XX*^{e} *siècle,* Paris, Gallimard, 1972.

Verma Shiv (ed.), *Bhagat Singh: On the path to liberation,* Chennai, Bharati Pusthakalyam, 2007.

Vidal Denis, *Violences et vérités. Un royaume du Rajasthan face au pouvoir colonial,* Paris, Éditions de l'EHESS, 1995.

Von Grünebaum Gustav E., *L'identité culturelle de l'Islam*, Paris, Gallimard, 1969.

Younis Sherif, "Marxisme et patriotisme dans les régimes militaires de libération nationale: les officiers libres et les "communistes égyptiens", *Cahiers d'histoire Revue d'histoire critique*, n°s 105–06, 2008, pp. 157–59.

Zachariah Mathew, *Revolution through reform. A comparison of Sarvodaya and Conscientization,* New Delhi, Vistaar Publications, 1988 (New York, Praeger Publishers, 1986).

Zarzoubrine Vladimir, *Le Tchékiste,* Paris, C. Bourgois, 1990.

Zubaida Sami, *Islam, the People and the State. Essays on Political Ideas and Movements in the Middle East,* London, I. B. Tauris, 1993.